Contents

Series Preface

The Steps to Success Activity Series is a breakthrough in skill instruction through the development of complete learning progressions—the *steps to success*. These *steps* help individuals quickly perform basic skills successfully and prepare them to acquire more advanced skills readily. At each step, individuals are encouraged to learn at their own pace and to integrate their new skills into the total action of the activity.

The unique features of the Steps to Success Activity Series are the result of comprehensive development—through analyzing existing activity books, incorporating the latest research from the sport sciences, and consulting with students, instructors, teacher educators, and administrators. This groundwork pointed up the need for three different types of books—for participants, instructors, and teacher educators—which we have created and together comprise the Steps to Success Activity Series.

This participant's book, *Nordic Skiing: Steps to Success*, is a self-paced, step-by-step guide that you can use as an instructional tool. The unique features of this participant's book include

- sequential illustrations that clearly show proper technique,
- helpful suggestions for detecting and correcting errors,
- excellent drill progressions with accompanying *Success Goals* for measuring performance, and
- checklists for rating technique.

Many of the activities in the Steps to Success Activity Series also have a comprehensive instructor's guide. However, one has not been developed for Nordic skiing.

The series textbook, *Instructional Design for Teaching Physical Activities* (Vickers, 1990), explains the *steps to success* model, which is the basis for the Steps to Success Activity Series. Teacher educators can use the series textbook in their professional preparation classes to help future teachers and coaches learn how to design effective physical activity programs in school, recreation, or community teaching and coaching settings.

After identifying the need for various texts, we refined the *steps to success* instructional design model and developed prototypes. Once these prototypes were fine-tuned, we carefully selected authors for the activities who were not only thoroughly familiar with their sports but also had years of experience in teaching them. Each author had to be known as a gifted instructor who understands the teaching of sport so thoroughly that he or she could readily apply the *steps to success* model.

Next, all of the manuscripts were carefully developed to meet the guidelines of the *steps to success* model. Then our production team, along with outstanding artists, created a highly visual, user-friendly series of books.

The result: The Steps to Success Activity Series is the premier sports instructional series available today.

This series would not have been possible without the contributions of the following:

- Dr. Rainer Martens, Publisher,
- Dr. Joan Vickers, instructional design expert,
- the staff of Human Kinetics Publishers, and
- the *many* students, teachers, coaches, consultants, teacher educators, specialists, and administrators who shared their ideas—and dreams.

Judy Patterson Wright
Series Editor

Looking for an inexpensive way to stay active and physically fit during cold weather? Let Nordic skiing lead you to a new appreciation of the outdoors in winter.

Many runners, bicyclists, and paddlers have chosen cross-country skiing for its cross-training benefits, because its aerobic value is high. People of all ages find it an appealing way to enjoy the winter landscape. The sport encourages the adventurer in you to emerge; it gets you to new places in the woods, because you easily and quickly glide past the locations to which you would normally hike. New discoveries await—in the landscape and within yourself! Let this book be your companion during cross-country explorations.

During the 1970s, an infant Nordic industry advertised the sport to newcomers with the slogan ''If you can walk, you can ski.'' It was a true but misleading statement, which led to lots of people walking on their skis! Getting started is easy, but skiing well is more challenging. Cross-country skiing can be more than shuffling; it can be an opportunity for you to glide on your skis with control and exhilaration. If you seek to truly cross-country ski, this book is for you.

As a long-time Nordic instructor, I believe in the benefits of qualified instruction to begin a sport properly. There is no substitute for the immediate feedback that a professionally trained observer can offer. But I also recognize that people are likely to practice their skills independently of a formal lesson, and important learning takes place during these practice periods if the practice is constructive. This book provides you with a clear, logical plan for self-directed learning.

None of the existing cross-country books provide a clear progression of activities for learning to ski. They may address important elements of technique and provide practice exercises for specific maneuvers, but the learner is left with an unclear understanding of what comes next in the process and, more importantly, on what type of terrain to practice. An overall game plan is missing.

Nordic Skiing: Steps to Success follows a very specific, orderly path that embodies the essence of ''cross-country'' skiing. The step-by-step approach is geared to the typical terrain that you

are likely to ski as a beginner and intermediate student. A basic learning sequence of flat terrain, uphills, and downhills is repeated at each difficulty level: beginner (gentle hills), early intermediate (very moderate steepness), intermediate (moderate steepness), and late intermediate (steep). The solid progression of activities lets you progress higher and higher—literally—and confidently handle more difficult terrain.

The book gives you options. You'll learn the most useful maneuvers for comfortably handling progressively more difficult terrain. This problem-solving approach is like the decision making necessary during a ski tour along a trail.

Because fundamental skiing skills form the basis for the exercises, new skiers can easily identify the key components of each move. Understanding the underlying skills eliminates the mystery from the move! You understand what is involved and how it should happen. And people who already ski get a clear prescription for any ills they find in their performance. A ski instructor or recreation leader can also use this book as a resource, whether for a 2-hour lesson or a day-long workshop. Use the material as you seek to increase your own understanding and share that knowledge with others.

The amount of time you spend on each step may differ slightly from estimates I've given (see Time Estimation Chart). It's important, too, to vary your learning and to know when to end the formal practice and loosen up with a ski tour. Touring is important because you build your fitness as well as test your good practice with real trail experiences. If you encounter any problems, you can return to the book to repeat any activities from the appropriate step. If not, you can progress to the next step, which will introduce a new maneuver or more difficult terrain. Successful skiers will blend the steps in the book with progressively longer ski tours on increasingly adventurous terrain.

I do have an agenda hidden behind the activities. I hope your learning is so enjoyable and rewarding that it encourages you to become a lifelong skier. Certainly cross-country skiing is one of the most popular activities for our aging population, partially because of its cardiovascular benefits. But as a masters skier, I am also enthralled with the grace and power of the sport, which makes my days on skis some of the most rewarding in my life. My goal is that you experience the same enjoyment and grow to love the sport.

I thank my husband, Bruce Lindwall, for his continued patience, humor, and technical assistance during the writing of this latest book. The numerous indoor demonstrations of ski technique made an essential contribution. I also must thank Denny Wilkins, journalist, teacher, and Nordic armchair athlete, whose friendship and endless support helped me through the tough spots.

Laurie Gullion

Step number	Skill or concept	Learning time	Skill category
1	Fundamental skills	15-90 minutes	Beginning
2	Diagonal striding	15-30 minutes	
3	Double poling	15 minutes	
4	No-pole skating	15-30 minutes	
5	Climbing and descending gentle hills	30-60 minutes	
6	Controlling speed with the wedge	15-60 minutes	
7	Changing direction with turns	1-3 hours	Early intermediate
8	Developing power in the tracks	1-3 hours	Intermediate
9	Uphill diagonal striding	15-60 minutes	
10	Telemark turn descents	1-3 hours	
11	V-skating uphill	1-3 hours	Late intermediate
12	Fine-tuned turning	1-3 hours	
13	Accelerated skating	1-3 hours	

Figure P.1 Time estimation chart.

Laurie Gullion leading a game for kids at a ski festival in Maine.

The Steps to Success Staircase

Let this staircase to enjoyable and efficient cross-country skiing help you achieve proficiency and confidence with a new endeavor. Cross-country skiing is an enticing sport, because it's as accessible as your backyard. By following the steps in this book, you can easily explore the trails in your neighborhood park or nearby forest or cross-country ski area.

At the top of the staircase is that ideal image of a cross-country skier who strides powerfully across the snow, balancing gracefully on each leg and gliding smoothly along. You begin by walking on skis, but skiing well involves a crucial middle step—sliding on skis, or more particularly, gliding along on one ski at a time as you move down the trail. These skills are the bridge to the grace and power of skating or gliding along the tracks. You can achieve a similar efficiency in your skiing by following each of the 13 steps presented in this book.

You'll learn about the different types of Nordic skiing in "The Cross-Country Skiing Renaissance" section in preparation for this exploration of traditional and modern ski techniques. Use the "Selecting Equipment" and "Preparing Your Body for Success" sections to select the right clothing and equipment as well as warm-up exercises. Then begin to climb the skills staircase, which will help you learn beginning, intermediate, and advanced cross-country maneuvers on flat and hilly terrain.

Each step establishes a solid base from which to move easily to the next level. Learning to cross-country ski is based on your ability to control your body and to remain balanced on your skis as the terrain and the snow conditions change. The first step is developing the basic skills inherent in skiing maneuvers. Later you will learn how to combine these skills in various ways to perform 22 cross-country moves.

Step 1 presents a series of activities that develop eight fundamental skills in cross-country skiing. These light activities help to loosen you up, physically and mentally, to prepare you for continued, relaxed practice, and they provide an important foundation for subsequent practice. Beginning with this section encourages successful learning and lets you experience improvement quickly. In fact, many of these warm-up activities are an appropriate beginning to any ski tour.

Each subsequent step helps you learn the skiing maneuvers that work best on specific terrain. Steps 2 to 4 get you moving efficiently on flat terrain through effective use of the arms and legs. Then Steps 5 to 7 introduce you to the ups and downs of gentle hills, with an emphasis on speed control and changing direction.

After you've achieved improved comfort on the hills, you'll naturally want to add more power to your skiing. Steps 8 and 9 explore intermediate moves, including skating, that move you quickly along the trail. Step 10 addresses the classic telemark turn, and Step 11 helps you to skate uphill efficiently. Advanced turning is introduced in Step 12, followed by accelerated skating across flat terrain in Step 13.

Follow the sequence of activities, because it is designed to build on earlier practice. But it is always appropriate to return to an earlier exercise, particularly one emphasizing a skill, for additional practice when you encounter difficulty. In fact, the solution to common skiing problems is often repeated practice of a specific skill, and you may be directed to an earlier "skills" exercise in Step 1 as a solution.

Follow this sequence each step of the way:

1. Read the explantion of what is covered in each step, why the step is important, and how to execute the maneuvers.
2. Follow the numbered illustrations (the Keys to Success), which clearly show how your body changes position throughout each maneuver. The Keys to Success illustrate each beginning stance during a "preparation" phase as well as the changing stances during "execution" and "transition" phases.
3. Review the common errors that may occur and the recommended corrections. Each usually identifies a key skill that may be missing in your performance. Let this section provide you with solutions to any problems that may develop with your skiing. You can return to the exercises in Step 1 at any time to strengthen a specific skill.
4. Read the directions and the Success Goals for each drill. Practice the exercises in order, because they are arranged in an easy-to-difficult sequence. Record your scores and compare them to the Success

Goals, which you need to meet before moving on. It's important to solidly develop the skills targeted in one drill before proceeding to the next.

5. After you reach the Success Goals for a step, ask an observer—a knowledgeable friend, instructor, or coach—to observe your progress. Your observer can use the Keys to Success as a checklist to evaluate your performance and the Errors and Corrections to solve any problems you may experience.

6. Repeat these procedures for each of the 13 Steps to Success. Then rate yourself using the "Rating Your Total Progress" section at the end of the book. Your rating will help you identify any areas that need further practice, and you can return to the appropriate step in the book for more work.

This book is an excellent tool to use after initial professional instruction. A directed lesson promotes "perfect" practice, with an instructor providing feedback and corrections before your body memorizes an inefficient action. Cross-country ski areas also offer excellent tracks and packed trails, which provide a more stable surface for learning.

Remember to give your body a chance to adjust to the demands you're placing on it. Short tours are better for beginners than all-day excursions. Breaking your own trails can be tiring because the deeper snow makes gliding and maneuverability more difficult. It's difficult to gauge your stamina when you're just learning this highly aerobic activity. Choose trails that periodically loop back to the lodge or trailhead so you have choices about when to quit for the day.

Select flat, open terrain initially, and stay on easy, beginner trails. Trails at ski areas are marked with the international symbols for degrees of difficulty. First follow the "green circle" trails with gentle grades and gradual curves. Then graduate to the more difficult "blue square" and "black diamond" trails when you have the skills to ski in control.

Watch better skiers whenever you can, particularly when you are following the practice activities in this book. The visual images of proficient skiers can give you the proper stances and timing to imitate. Visualization is an important strategy in learning physical skills, because the mental imagery does help your body achieve the right rhythm. And skiing behind or beside an excellent skier provides even stronger practice for people who like to watch and do at the same time. Ask your local ski area or library about the many excellent videotapes of dynamic cross-country skiers.

Enjoy your step-by-step progress as you experience the satisfaction of learning to cross-country ski. It's a healthy, lifetime activity that can invigorate your appreciation for the outdoors in winter.

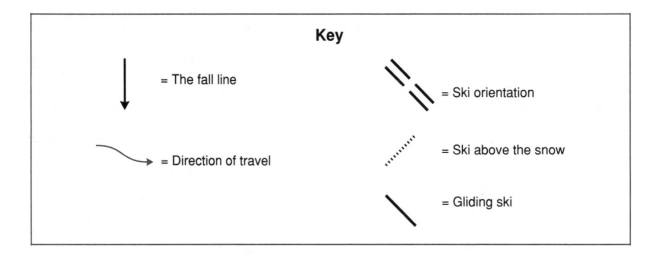

The Cross-Country Skiing Renaissance

Cross-country skiing originated in ancient Scandinavia, where the Norse people adapted to the rigors of their wintry homeland by using skis to travel, hunt, and defend themselves from hostile invaders. The earliest known record of a skier is a faded petroglyph, dating to 2000 B.C., on a rock wall in Norway. It features the shadowy form of a person on long, narrow skis, the length of the stout boards almost twice the figure's height (see Figure 1).

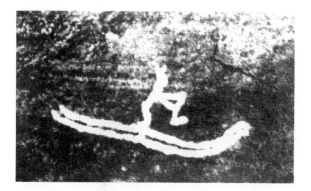

Figure 1 Cross-country skiing as a mode of transportation 4,000 years ago.

Skiing has a venerable history as an efficient mode of transport in snowy lands, whether the rolling plains of the northern Arctic or the steeper mountains of the European Alps and the American West. A look at skiing's history shows that ancient, functional techniques have resurfaced in the last 2 decades as spectacular innovations in the sport. But modern cross-country skiing is really a recreation of old skiing forms.

Long ago, the Norse hunters made the earliest design modifications to their skis and actually used a technique similar to today's marathon skate. They glided on one long ski and pushed themselves along with a shorter, skating ski for greater speed. To carve their unwieldy skis in a wide arc through the snow, they also developed the distinctive telemark turn, which takes its name from the Telemark region of Norway. The free-heeled nature of Nordic equipment allowed skiers to drop into a low, stable curtsy for good control while turning their long skis.

Scandinavian immigrants popularized cross-country skiing in the United States when they moved to this country in the 19th century. Although skiing still served as transportation through mountain passes in winter, it also began to emerge as a popular recreational activity. Western miners, eager for excitement in remote camps in the Rockies, developed camp teams and staged downhill races with gold in the winner's purse. In the 1880s, a significant design development changed the character of the sport and ushered in the era of modern skiing that we know today. When Sondre Nordheim of Norway developed birch-rope heel straps for skis, he spearheaded another evolution in technique. His tighter bindings improved control and allowed narrower, quicker turns. So did shorter skis and poles, which enabled skiers to turn with their skis in a parallel position. The christie turn was born and named after the Norwegian capital city of Oslo, also known as Christiana.

These advances in equipment created a distinction between Alpine (downhill) and Nordic (cross-country) skiing, which evolved as separate sports. Early in the 20th century, a small population of skiers organized ski clubs, sponsored competitions, and opened instructional schools. By 1934, the first ski lift, near Woodstock, Vermont, eliminated arduous hill climbing and made the sport more attractive. But the advent of World War II signaled the emergence of downhill skiing as a major industry.

In Colorado at Camp Hale, the famous 10th Mountain Division trained on skis to handle the rigors of conflict in the European Alps. After the war, the ski troops returned to civilian life and used their expertise to begin the first major ski resorts in this country. They swiftly refined the sport with an explosion of technological advances in equipment, particularly ski lifts, that firmly established the "downhill" industry. This Alpine style of skiing drew its name from the steep Alps of Europe, whereas the Nordic style remembered with its name its Scandinavian origins, where the ups and downs of skiing were (and still are) a part of daily life.

During the 1970s, skiers looked to a cheaper alternative to downhill skiing: Cross-country skiing experienced a renaissance. With a rising interest in aerobic fitness, the American public saw the sport as a natural complement to running and biking—another way to stay in shape in another season. Bill Koch won America's first Olympic medal in Nordic skiing at the 1976 Olympics, and by 1982, with Koch at the helm, the Americans emerged as strong contenders in the World Cup races, historically dominated by Scandinavians.

As Nordic competition intensified, racers discovered an alternative to the classic diagonal stride, which had been the dominant cross-country technique. As wax wore off their racing skis, they resorted to skating moves to propel themselves along the track. Although these maneuvers were initially viewed as too energy intensive, racers were nonetheless thrilled about their speed and trained intensively to skate the long marathons.

The first of the new skating moves was the marathon skate, a half-skate maneuver like that of the ancient Norse hunters. Its effectiveness led to experimentation with full skating maneuvers akin to ice skating, with many poling variations to spice up the mix. The 1980s saw two types of Nordic skiing evolve: classical (traditional) skiing in the tracks and freestyle (skating) out of the tracks on wide, groomed trails.

Meanwhile, skiers were also leaving the groomed trails of downhill and cross-country ski areas to travel into the forests of New England and the back bowls of the West. They began to combine the virtues of their Nordic equipment with the benefits of Alpine gear. Metal edges and wider Alpine skis increased control, while softer boots and free-heeled Nordic bindings expanded the range of terrain to explore. Skiers rediscovered the telemark and added christies and parallel turns to this mixed bag of turning strategies when they returned to lift-serviced areas to spawn a new generation of telemark, or Nordic downhill, skiers.

CROSS-COUNTRY SKIING TODAY

Now cross-country skiing has diverged into three different areas—classical, freestyle, and Nordic downhill—that are strongly interrelated and rooted in the same skiing skills. Skiing is skiing, and all forms rely upon the same principles of balance; skiers adapt these underlying skills to suit the differences in equipment and terrain that characterize each type of cross-country skiing.

This book addresses classical, freestyle, and Nordic downhill maneuvers on light cross-country equipment. You will learn how to execute these moves to enjoy skiing at cross-country ski areas and local forests and parks.

Classical Skiing

The most common image in cross-country skiing is the skier who strides sturdily across the snow, arms and legs outstretched in the classic pose associated with the diagonal stride (see Figure 2). It is the most common move used by cross-country skiers, especially those who are learning to ski, because its initial similarity to walking offers great security. However, the diagonal stride transforms walking on skis into the exhilaration of gliding along a track.

Figure 2 The diagonal stride is the most common classical maneuver.

Today, "classical" skiing refers to the "preskating" moves that we associate with traditional cross-country skiing:

- Diagonal stride
- Double poling
- Kick double pole
- Uphill diagonal stride
- Herringbone

It also means the use of skis with a patterned or waxable base that provides traction. Each time skiers stride forward, they "set" their wax or base into the snow to get a good grip. Because of this momentary disruption in forward glide, classical skiing tends to be slower than skating.

In competition, classical races prohibit skating and dictate the use of the diagonal stride. Abandoned during the impassioned rise of freestyle competition, classical racing is now experiencing renewed popularity. Many racers enjoy this style of racing, because it represents a different challenge from skating and improves overall conditioning. In international competition, the races are now divided into classical and freestyle events.

Freestyle Skiing

Experienced skiers enjoy skating because it is a fast, powerful form of skiing. The distinctive V-shaped formation of the skis lets a skier push off the ski edge for good traction (see Figure 3). Because this eliminates the need for grip wax to obtain traction, the entire ski is waxed for maximum glide. Consequently, skating maneuvers allow a skier to move faster across the snow.

Figure 3 The V-shaped formation aids traction and increases speed.

Today, ''freestyle'' skiing refers to these maneuvers:

- Marathon skate
- No-pole skating
- Diagonal V
- V1
- V2
- V2 Alternate

Skating maneuvers force skiers to glide on one ski at a time, which can be a challenging undertaking for a new skier, who may prefer the security of initially shuffling across the snow in the diagonal stride. But beginners who commit themselves to learning basic skating moves will become aggressive skiers sooner. They may risk

falling more frequently at the outset, but they will improve their one-ski balance more rapidly than the classical skier.

Skating is designed for groomed trails at a cross-country ski area, where skiers can skim across a hard surface. Loose, deep snow will fatigue a skater and make the experience frustrating. Many ski areas groom wide skating lanes because the general public is increasingly interested in freestyle technique.

Nordic Downhill

All cross-country skiers use downhill moves, but a new hybrid sport known as Nordic downhill skiing mixes the best of the Nordic and Alpine worlds. Skiers use metal-edged skis that are lighter than Alpine gear but offer more control than Nordic touring equipment. A heavier boot and a tougher Nordic binding leave the skier with free heels to execute telemark turns on the same terrain as Alpine skiers (see Figure 4). Steep, thrilling descents are the province of these skiers, as are backcountry explorations away from lift-serviced areas.

Figure 4 Nordic downhill skiing uses a telemark turn in the backcountry.

Also known as ''telemark'' skiing, the sport is actually a blend of many moves beyond the telemark turn:

- Wedge
- Wedge turn

- Wedge christie
- Parallel turn
- Telemark turn
- Skate turn

This book adapts these moves to the use of lighter touring equipment at cross-country ski areas. But you can also adapt these maneuvers to the style of Nordic downhill skiing used at lift-serviced areas.

VERSATILE SKIING

Because the three Nordic disciplines share the same basic skills as a foundation, beginners can easily explore elements of each sport. The cross-over benefits are enormous, because the skills reinforced in one area are transferable to another. This blend allows quick development in each area, and the new skier can experience enormous rewards in one season.

The most versatile cross-country skiers are those who have experienced the three different types of Nordic disciplines. Learning a variety of moves lets a skier handle different snow conditions, including deep powder, hard pack, crusty snow, and ice as well as varied terrain.

Skating's reliance on one-ski balance enables a skier to perform a better diagonal stride, because the ability to glide longer on each ski improves greatly. Nordic downhill skiing increases comfort with speed and speed control, which can make skiers more aggressive when they return to lighter equipment. Skiers learn to generate power efficiently and subtly in classical skiing, and this ability can make them smoother with their skating and downhill skiing.

Selecting Equipment

Selecting the proper equipment improves your comfort and control when learning how to cross-country ski. Equipment that fits securely allows you to control the skis precisely and feel more confident in performing the moves; poorly fitting equipment can frustrate you and diminish your learning. It's generally best not to borrow from a well-meaning friend, unless the equipment is the right size. Errors become difficult to correct when you are unsure whether your equipment or your body creates the problem.

Think of your boot–binding–ski combination as a communication system. Your feet must fit securely in the boots, which send messages to the bindings, which send messages to the skis. If any part of the system is loose, then the effectiveness of the message is diminished. Boots should fit securely without being too tight or too loose, the binding should hold the boot securely, and the skis should match your physical size.

But equally important is choosing equipment that suits the type of cross-country activities that interest you. Is enjoying the outdoors your primary objective? Is touring on woodland trails your main goal? Is skiing a major part of a winter fitness program? Is citizen's racing your motivation? Match your equipment to your goals.

Despite the specialized equipment available today, it is still possible to find a multipurpose set of equipment that will allow you to learn a variety of maneuvers. However, if you are interested primarily in one form of cross-country skiing, then choose equipment specially suited to that endeavor.

Beginners can rent equipment from local shops or ski areas to discover the virtues of different brands. Today most ski areas also have skating equipment available for rent. Once you have learned how to size your own equipment and have experienced different models, you are ready to purchase your own equipment.

CLASSICAL EQUIPMENT

Light touring equipment is used for groomed tracks at ski areas or ungroomed snow in local parks and forests. Most equipment sold today fits this category. The medium-width skis allow you to "float" more easily on the snow, and the ski design allows good straight-ahead tracking

and turning. The skis are "softer" so that skiers can get good traction with minimal effort.

Classical racers choose a higher performance ski, narrower in width, to reduce drag in the tracks and to enhance glide. Outside of groomed tracks, a narrower ski will tend to cut and sink through the snow. This classical ski tends to be a "stiffer," responsive ski matched to the more dynamic style of racers.

Skiers interested in classical and freestyle skiing can choose a higher performance classical ski that they can wax to suit the type of skiing. Many companies now manufacture "combi" skis and boots especially for skiers who want their equipment to perform many functions.

FREESTYLE EQUIPMENT

Some notable differences in skating equipment distinguish it from classical equipment. Because skaters use the inside edges of their skis repeatedly in a V-shaped formation, reinforced sides reduce the stresses of edging on the ski. Increased lateral stability in the boot-binding system is another major innovation prompted by skating, and it allows the skier to better control edging.

Beginning skaters can choose a wider width ski that offers a more secure platform to balance on when gliding. Experienced skaters often choose a narrower width for lightness, less resistance against the snow, and faster glide.

A big difference in freestyle skiing is longer and stiffer poles. The extra length helps the skier get the pole plant behind the V-shaped skis to avoid tripping over the poles (one of the most common experiences in beginning skating). The longer length also extends the duration of the poling phase, which enhances glide.

Nordic Downhill Equipment

A key difference in Nordic downhill equipment is the addition of metal edges to a heavier, wider ski for greater control on steep descents. Telemark equipment is a blend of Alpine and Nordic gear, and the degree to which it resembles either is a function of the environment.

Skiers attracted to high-speed downhill skiing at lift-serviced areas should choose heavier telemark equipment with stiffer boots and rugged bindings. The equipment begins to resemble Alpine gear. Shorter Alpine-style poles are appropriate to aid in turning on this steeper terrain.

Skiers interested in lighter backcountry touring across cross-country terrain should choose lighter-weight telemark equipment and boots for increased comfort. Many use adjustable poles, which can be altered for climbing uphills and then descending. This equipment more closely resembles Nordic gear and would be very appropriate for all maneuvers introduced in this book.

SKI SELECTION

The first choice for a beginner is deciding between a waxable or a waxless ski. A *waxable* ski needs a thin coat of wax applied to its base to match the day's snow conditions. It allows improved traction, because you can tailor the ski to suit changing conditions, even during a day tour. You can also wax this ski for faster glide, which is pleasing to skiers who are feeling increasingly comfortable on their skis.

A *waxless* or ''no-wax'' ski has a patterned base that provides the traction. You can rub your hand along the ski's underside to feel the pattern created in the manufacturing process. The ski requires little care and suits people who do not enjoy ski preparation. It tends to be a slower ski, because the pattern provides more resistance against the snow.

Infrequent skiers like waxless skis because they can enjoy the outdoors with little fuss. These skis are appropriate at ski areas, and you can also use them for light backcountry touring, especially if they are wide enough for you to break your own trail. Most cross-country skiers use a waxless ski, because it offers convenient, enjoyable participation.

Those who ski frequently or want better performance are wise to choose the waxable ski for its versatility. The more you ski, the more you will want superior equipment to improve your performance. Skiers with an interest in skating should avoid a waxless ski, because the patterned base on an edged ski digs into the snow and slows glide. This disruption can also be jarring and create balance problems for the beginner.

Once you have decided on the environment in which you are most likely to ski, several other factors affect your choice of skis: camber, length, width, and flex.

Camber

All skis have some *camber*, which is the arc or bow in the middle of a ski (see Figure 5). Camber affects the amount of force needed to bring the midsection in contact with the snow. ''Softer'' camber takes less force from an individual, and skis designed for beginning to intermediate skiers often have a softer camber. ''Stiffer'' camber takes more force to press the midsection against the snow, and athletic skiers are wise to choose a ski with stiffer camber.

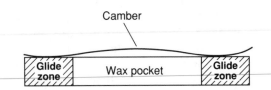

Figure 5 Camber of ski.

Camber becomes important on light touring skis in relation to the *wax pocket* in the ski's midsection. The wax pocket is the area under and forward of the feet where skiers apply wax to get good grip. When you walk or stride on skis, you move from ski to ski and press the wax pocket of each ski against the snow to move forward. When you glide down a hill with your feet side by side, you distribute your weight equally between the skis, which lifts the wax pockets off the snow. The proper camber is soft enough to easily engage the wax pocket when you stride forward and stiff enough to prevent the wax pocket from dragging when you glide downhill.

Your weight can also affect the necessary degree of camber. Heavier people need a stiffer camber to support their weight along the ski. Lighter people need a softer camber, which allows them to flatten the ski against the snow for good traction.

The final consideration is skiing ability. Experienced skiers usually have a more dynamic skiing style; they can depress the ski more forcefully than a beginner and need a stiffer camber that responds well to their athleticism. Beginners, usually more passive with their technique, need a softer camber that allows them to get good grip easily with minimal effort.

Length

Your height and weight determine the appropriate length of your skis, and your weight can be the more important criterion. Ski length also varies with the type of cross-country skiing. Many personal factors affect a good choice, but the following general guidelines are helpful.

Classical. Classical skis should reach approximately to your wrist when your arm extends above your head (see Figure 6), but this measurement also depends upon other considerations (particularly if you have long arms). Generally, a lighter person can select a shorter than average ski for easier maneuverability. Some manufacturers recommend 30 centimeters over head height for men and 25 centimeters for women, assuming women are lighter in weight.

Figure 6 Classical (a) and freestyle (b) ski length.

Freestyle. Freestyle skis are usually sized 10 centimeters shorter than your classical length, but experienced skiers like a slightly longer skating ski in looser snow conditions (again, see Figure 6).

Width

Ski width affects how well the ski performs in different snow conditions. A wider ski provides greater stability and control, and it is the better choice in ungroomed, out-of-track conditions. A wider tip helps a ski to float more easily in deep snow. A narrower ski tends to cut or sink through the snow, but it travels with less resistance along a hardened track.

Nordic skis are classified by their waist (middle) measurement:

- Racing skis   44-45 mm
- Light touring skis   45-47 mm
- Touring   49-54 mm
- Nordic downhill   approximately 55 mm

Width can vary along a ski's length from tip to tail and gives the ski a particular shape. The differences in width at the tip, waist, and tail of the ski determine whether *sidecut* is present. A ski shaped like an hourglass—with a narrower waist and a wider tip and tail—has sidecut.

The greater the sidecut, the easier the ski turns. Edging a ski reverses the camber so that the ski creates an arc against the snow. The entire edge of the ski follows the arc to turn the ski. Nordic downhill skis generally have good sidecut for ease in turning.

Classical and freestyle racing skis can also have *parallel* cut, in which the width is relatively uniform along the length (see Figure 7, a and b). Most suitable for groomed snow, skis without sidecut tend to track in a straighter line rather than turn easily or hold an edge well.

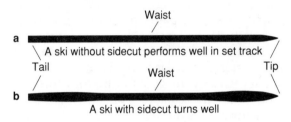

Figure 7 Parallel (a) and sidecut (b) ski widths.

Historically, sidecut was the most important ingredient in determining how well a stiff, wooden ski turned. But new production methods now make a ski's flex a greater influence.

Flex

The degree to which a ski bends is its *flex*, and a ski can flex in two ways: along its length and around its axis, which is called *torsional rigidity*. Skis are often characterized as having soft, medium, or hard flex (or stiffness).

To test flex, you can pull back on the tip or push the tail against the floor. The ski should bend evenly against this pressure and curve gradually rather than curve more sharply at a specific point. You can also twist the ski, as if wringing out a towel, to test its torsional rigidity.

Synthetic materials and modern construction methods allow a single ski to have different flexes along its length for improved performance, and the flexes have a great impact upon the ski's tracking and turning ability. A softer tip will act as a shock absorber and ride up and over changes in the track or snow. In track skis, a soft tip not only increases shock absorption but also aids turning. A stiff tip lets a mountaineering ski hold an edge on ice. A skating ski is torsionally stiff to provide support while edging, but the ski tip is usually moderately soft to prevent it from turning inward or outward excessively.

Tail flex is usually stiffer than tip flex, to hold the arc of a turn and to prevent the ski from "washing out." This ability to hold an edge is especially important in Nordic downhill and skating skis.

TESTING YOUR SKIS

The trick is selecting a pair of skis that are neither too stiff nor too soft—both in overall flex and in camber. With high-performance classical and freestyle skis, the ski manufacturer provides you with guidelines to the appropriate flex for your weight. A simple paper test can fine-tune the process further.

Find a hard surface (not a rug) on which to test the skis. If the skis have mounted bindings, you can wear your boots to perform the test. If not, find the balance point of the skis by balancing each ski on your finger. Then place your toes about an inch behind that point to simulate actual use. Stand with your feet side by side as if you were gliding downhill.

Ask a friend to slip a piece of paper under the ski and move it forward and backward as far as possible. This area shows the part of the ski that will be raised off the snow when you are gliding on equally weighted skis. It usually reaches from behind the heel to approximately a foot in front of the toes.

If this zone is smaller than the recommended area, then the skis are too soft. The wax pocket will be dragging on the snow, slowing you down continually and wearing off the wax or the patterned base. You will be able to climb easily, but the skis will be too slow and, ultimately, unenjoyable.

Now balance on one foot with the paper under the ski. The paper should be trapped by the pressure of the ski against the floor. This action corresponds to the weight transfer that occurs when you stride across the snow.

If the paper moves a lot, the skis are too stiff. You will be unable to press the wax pocket against the snow unless you pounce on the ski with each step. Hill climbing especially will be too frustrating, but even striding in the tracks, you will have poor traction and too much slipping.

More advanced skiers using stiffer skis may get some paper movement when performing this test. If you are willing to "grow" into your skis and your ultimate goal is serious recreational skiing or racing, then a stiffer ski is a good choice.

BOOTS AND BINDINGS

These two items need to be considered a unit in today's market, because of technological advances in modern boot-binding systems. Cross-country equipment has matured beyond the still very serviceable "three-pin" setup into new systems that offer increased control and responsiveness. More specialized equipment is now available for each type of cross-country skiing.

Your best strategy is finding a comfortable boot that fits your foot properly without being too tight or too loose. The fit should be similar to the comfort of a running shoe. When you stride forward, the boot shouldn't pinch your foot where the boot "breaks" over your toes. Once you've found the right boot for your foot, then you often have to choose the binding that matches that system.

Classical boots and bindings are available in recreational and racing models, and they are often lower cut for comfort (see Figure 8). A person who intends to pursue a lot of out-of-track skiing might prefer a higher-cut boot with a snow cuff. A softer flex plate in the binding allows your heel to lift off the ski and over your toes comfortably to stride forward.

Figure 8 Classical ski boot and binding.

Skating boots have evolved into higher-cut models with reinforced sides that help to support the foot laterally (see Figure 9). The reinforcement increases control during edging. The flex plates in the bindings tend to be stiffer than classical ones, to quickly "return" the ski to the foot during skating.

New "combi" models let a skier enjoy both skating and striding. The boot has an above-the-ankle cut with some stiffening, but it is soft enough to flex forward for striding.

Figure 9 Skating boot and binding.

Light backcountry equipment can provide a very good system for all types of skiing without the expense of specialized equipment. It lacks some of the superior performance of specialized gear, but it can provide good control in classical, freestyle, and moderate telemark skiing in ungroomed terrain (see Figure 10).

Figure 10 A light backcountry boot and binding.

POLES

Ski poles function as an extension of your arms, and they should match your body size as well as the type of skiing. Poling supplements the power provided by your legs; beginners generate a small amount of force from their poles, but improving skiers use their poles more dynamically to aid propulsion.

Poles range from recreational to high-performance models where increased stiffness and strength are necessary to handle the stresses of aggressive poling. A basic fiberglass pole is enough for a casual skier, but more advanced skiers will appreciate a stronger design. A pole that bends excessively under your poling thrust isn't stiff enough to efficiently transfer your power into forward momentum. Much effort is lost as the pole absorbs the thrust.

Classical poles are now measured to the top of the shoulder rather than to the underarm (see Figure 11). As skating evolved, skiers experienced the benefits of a longer poling phase and discovered it also improved their overall power during diagonal striding.

Skating poles are longer than classical poles and need to be stiffer. The "mouth" rule is a good guideline in selecting the proper length (again, see Figure 11). The pole should reach between your mouth and your chin. This length gets the tips behind your V-shaped skis and extends the poling phase.

Figure 11 Classic pole (a), Nordic downhill pole (b), and skating pole (c).

Backcountry skiers need a little of both types of poles—a longer length when striding and a shorter length when descending hills. For that reason, adjustable poles work well, because the internal locking mechanism adjusts easily to shorten or lengthen the poles. For downhill skiing, your arm should form a right angle at the elbow when you plant the pole (again, see Figure 11). However, many backcountry skiers simply use a longer pole for striding and avoid pole plants on the downhills.

Soft snow requires rounder, larger pole baskets to prevent the shaft from sinking. Assymetrical baskets, smaller in front of the shaft than behind, work well on groomed snow and prevent the pole from popping prematurely off the hard surface.

Correct pole grip is crucial to efficient skiing. Wear the pole strap like a bracelet with your hand *above* the webbing as you grab the pole. When you extend the pole behind your body, relax your hand enough to release the pole slightly while your thumb and forefinger still control it. Adjust the strap snugly enough that the top of the grip rests in the V of your hand during the release (see Figure 12). The secure fit allows you to recover the pole quickly when your arm swings forward for the next plant.

Figure 12 Correct pole grip.

WAXING

Waxable skis outperform waxless in most snow conditions, and enthusiastic recreational skiers will enjoy the superior speed of waxable skis. Learning how to wax them properly takes an awareness of wax types, snow conditions, and temperature. A certain amount of experimentation is necessary, and even expert skiers have days when they haven't anticipated weather changes properly. But the reward of a properly waxed ski is worth an exploration of waxing basics.

Skiers wax for two purposes: grip and glide. *Grip* wax is stickier, actually grips the snow, and gives you traction to move forward. *Glide* wax is more slippery, reduces friction against the snow, and promotes sliding.

Skis have grip and glide zones. Skaters wax the entire ski with glide wax to promote sliding. The whole ski actually functions as a glide zone. The skiers melt and iron in the glide wax for a good bond; then they scrape off the excess to promote optimal sliding.

Classical skiers wax for optimum grip and glide; they wax the tips and tails for gliding (since only these portions touch the snow on descents) and the wax pocket (which presses against the snow during striding) for gripping. They apply glide wax to the tips and tails, and they leave the wax pocket bare for the application of grip wax. The wax pocket can vary be-

tween skis, so use the paper test (explained on page 8) to find this zone on your skis.

The next step is determining which wax is appropriate for the day's conditions. Understanding the relationship between the wax and the snow is helpful.

Snow Conditions

Weather greatly affects the shape of snow crystals. Fresh, cold snow resembles our childhood cutouts of snow crystals—sharp, jagged edges like carpet tacks. Old, warm snow loses its original shape and softens during melting and refreezing—into round, smooth curves like ball bearings.

An inverse relationship exists between the snow and the wax to achieve a good bond. New jagged crystals need a smooth, hard wax; old, rounded snow needs a softer, tackier wax for a good bond (see Figure 13, a and b).

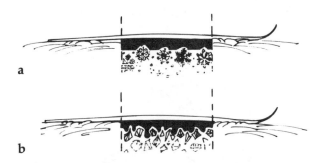

Figure 13 New, abrasive snow needs a hard grip wax (a) old, warm snow needs a softer, tackier wax (b).

The right wax offers enough grip to move forward, and, most importantly, it also releases the snow crystals to prevent ice buildup. A wax that is too hard doesn't give enough grip; this will be apparent when you begin to slip going uphill. A wax that is too soft holds the crystals, and soon you will have an icy layer on the ski base that requires repeated scraping.

Hard and Soft Waxes

There are two types of grip waxes: *hard* wax for newer snow and *soft*, or *klister*, wax for older snow. The hard wax looks like a fat crayon and, in fact, gets rubbed into the wax pocket the way you would color with crayons. A final vigorous rubbing with a cork smoothes the hard wax to avoid excessive grab and makes it look almost transparent.

Klisters come in squeeze tubes and often have their own plan for when to ooze (in the pocket of your pack) or freeze (when your hands are too cold to warm the tube). They need to be warm to be applied effectively in a thin stream or little dabs along the wax pocket, without slopping over into the depression running the length of the ski. Take the plastic klister spreader and gently smooth out the klister along the base. Then let the klister harden before you ski.

You might need a torch or iron to heat the klister and completely spread it along the ski base. Heating also provides a better bond between the wax and the ski. For skiing in icy tracks covered with a light dusting of snow, you would be wise to apply a hard wax over the klister to prevent icing. Let the klister cool before adding the final layer of kick wax.

Choosing the Right Wax

Don't get bewildered by the array of colored waxes from which to choose. Both grip and glide waxes come in a variety of primary and secondary colors that are matched to temperature. Remember this basic guideline: Choose warmer colors (yellow, red) on warm days and cooler colors (blue, green) on cold days. Purple is an intermediate color (a mix of blue and red) for middle-range temperatures.

If you can't remember the color scale at first, it doesn't matter! Each hard-wax can or klister tube has a temperature range marked on the container. Choose the color that matches the temperature, apply it, and then *test it* before heading out on a tour. Even the best skiers make an educated guess, based upon the age of the snow and the temperature, and then ski on the wax to see if it works.

If a hard wax seems slow, scrap it off and apply the next colder wax to reduce drag. If you aren't getting enough grip, the wax needs to be warmer to improve traction. If you are skiing all day, you often need to add warmer waxes as the day warms up. You can add the warmer color over the first layer, which provides a bond for the new wax. Keep waxing simple at the beginning, before you explore more advanced ski preparation with those who like to prep their skis for hours!

A final word on cleaning skis is necessary. Clean them as little as possible with wax solvents, which are toxic (but efficient). Use plastic gloves to avoid skin contact with the solvent, and apply the solvent in a well-ventilated area away from open flames. It's a highly flammable substance. Good alternatives are newly developed wax removers that are billed as nontoxic and better for your health and safety.

Even better is to scrape the wax from your skis or to heat the layers with a torch and wipe them off. A substantial amount of the wax, even klisters, can be removed in this manner with little or no residue. Then you can simply begin the waxing process from this point. However, a particularly messy ski will probably benefit from a thorough cleaning.

CLOTHING

Cross-country skiing is an active sport where skiers are usually too warm rather than too cold! The ups and downs of cross-country terrain usually offer a good mix of climbing and descending that keeps a person very warm. A recreational skier who covers 5 miles in an hour has burned 500 to 600 calories.

For classical and freestyle skiing, the best choices are loose layers of clothing that you can add or shed easily to regulate your body temperature. Loose clothing allows unrestricted arm and leg swing. Stretch fabrics like lycra provide great freedom of movement but offer very little warmth because they are designed for very active skiers.

Avoid bulky parkas that can get too hot. Many lighter layers provide good insulation, and you can remove them easily before you perspire much within your clothes. Clothing wet with perspiration will cool you during long descents and rest periods.

A three-layered system works well: (a) a wicking layer of long underwear, polypropylene or silk, close to the skin, that moves perspiration away from the body into other layers; (b) an insulating layer in the middle, such as a wool sweater, to provide warmth; and (c) a weatherproof layer on the outside to shed wind, rain, or snow. This same system is also appropriate for Nordic downhill skiers with the addition of a parka for greater warmth when riding ski lifts.

Experiment with layering systems to discover what works best for you, because people differ in metabolism. A "colder" person will need different clothing than one who runs "warm." And as you become a more efficient skier, you may find that your clothing needs change. You may need more clothing to keep warm, because your "motor" isn't working as hard to ski.

Preparing Your Body for Success

Cross-country skiing is a highly aerobic activity that exercises the entire body; physiologists view it as one of the best total-body conditioners. Because skiers climb hills as well as descend them, the cardiovascular benefits of the sport are extremely high. The sport provides an excellent way to achieve superb lifelong health and fitness. For many, it is an important winter component of an annual fitness program.

You determine the demands of the sport through your choice of terrain and the intensity with which you participate. Recreational participation and touring differ greatly from racing. Racers can burn more than 1,000 calories an hour in marathons, while touring skiers can use approximately 500 to 600 calories an hour when skiing consistently. Pace yourself, and match your conditioning to the intensity of your activity.

If you are new to cross-country skiing, many of your daily activities have conditioned you naturally to the sport. Walking to work or classes, running, hiking, skating, and bicycling are good ways to strengthen your legs as well as improve your heart and lungs. Swimming is an effective way to strengthen your upper body for poling. Hiking or jogging with ski poles is a great specific conditioner for the more serious recreational participant or racer.

WARMING UP

Before every skiing experience, perform a series of warm-up exercises that physically prepare your body for the activity. These exercises improve blood flow to your muscles, stretch them gently, and generally "wake them up" for more strenuous performance on cross-country terrain. In addition, the exercises also help orient you to the skiing equipment and, most importantly, develop your balance.

Individuals vary in the length and intensity of their warm-ups, depending upon their conditioning, but a good general guideline in skiing is approximately 15 minutes, until you feel comfortably warm in your outdoor clothing. If you are sweating heavily, then you may be overdressed and may need to remove a layer of clothing.

First choose warm-up exercises that elevate your heart rate, which increases blood flow to the muscles and guards against injury. Then begin flexibility exercises. Finish with the skills

exercises in Step 1 to complete a total warm-up period of a half hour.

Exercises to Elevate Your Heart Rate

Choose one or more of the following exercises. When you perspire slightly and breathe deeply without gasping, your muscles are warmed sufficiently and your heart and lungs are ready to perform.

Pole Hiking: Swing your ski poles naturally while you walk around the parking lot or along the road (without wearing skis). Then jog gently for 2 to 3 minutes until you begin to breathe deeply. You'll begin to swing the ski poles faster as you change to jogging.

Ski Jogging in Place: With skis on, start to move gently from ski to ski, barely lifting each ski from the snow, and keeping your feet a foot apart. When you become more comfortable transferring your weight from ski to ski, begin to jog in place. Increase the intensity of the jogging for 30 to 60 seconds.

Jumping Jacks: With skis on, jump between a narrower stance and a wider stance for 30 to 60 seconds, until you begin to breathe deeply. Without poles, you can also raise and lower your arms at the same time. Keep your legs flexed at the ankles and knees to absorb the impact and edge the skis.

Sidestepping: Step sideways, keeping the skis parallel so the tips don't overlap. Begin to step faster and faster without becoming unbalanced. Change directions, beginning slowly and then stepping faster. Repeat without looking at your ski tips, and try to feel when the skis are parallel.

Flexibility Exercises

Cross-country skiers need to increase the range of motion of their arms, legs, and torso for better performance. Increased flexibility in the joints enables you to be more powerful and flowing in your skiing. The ability to flex and extend your limbs lets you "springload" them for more power and loosen them for increased absorption of bumps and dips in terrain.

The best approach is static stretching, which avoids jerking and tearing the muscles. Stretch gently and smoothly to maintain your balance. Hold the stretch for the recommended amount of time, unless you feel insecure on your skis in the static position. Return to a neutral position (with flexed ankles and knees) to regain your balance, and begin the stretch again.

Trunk

Torso Rotation: Stand comfortably on your skis, and hold the mid shafts of your poles with both hands. Rotate your torso until the poles are parallel with your outside ski. Hold the stretch for 30 seconds. Repeat in the other direction.

Hips

Hip Swivels: Stand comfortably on your skis. Use your spine as a central axis and swivel your hips around the axis. Let your shoulders follow your hips at first for a greater range of motion. Hold the stretch for 15 seconds. Then try to swivel your hips without moving your shoulders. Put your hands on each shoulder to help isolate the hip action. Hold the stretch for 15 seconds, and repeat in the other direction.

Legs

Leg Swings: Let your leg swing backward and forward with little bend at the knee. Use your poles for balance as you swing the leg for 15 seconds. Let your hip swing also, so the pelvis rotates back and forth. When your leg is fully extended frontward and backward, hold each stretch for 5 to 10 seconds if you can. Keep the swinging ski parallel to the ski on the ground. Repeat with the other leg.

Quadriceps Stretch: From a neutral standing position, slide one ski forward and bend that knee. Sink deeply until you feel the stretch in your other leg. Try to hold the stretch for 10 seconds (your balance might get wobbly). Repeat with the other leg.

Groin

Side Lunge: Take a large step sideways, and move your weight over the ski to balance securely. Bend your knee and ankle slowly to lower your body, until you feel a stretch in the other leg. Hold for 15 seconds. Repeat with the other leg.

Lower Back

Deep Bows: Stand with your feet comfortably apart and knees slightly bent. Slowly bend over and grasp your legs as low as possible. Hold for 30 seconds.

Ankles

Ankle Flexes: From a standing position, bend your ankles until you can feel your shins pressing against the boot tongues. Do not let your heels rise off the skis. Hold for 15 seconds. Relax in an upright position. Repeat. Try to flex the ankles more strongly to sink lower.

Arms

Alternate Arm Swings: Extend one arm forward to shoulder height. Extend the other arm backward as high as possible. Alternate swinging your arms downward past your thighs in an arc bringing one arm rearward and the other arm forward. Raise the rearward arm as high as possible and hold the stretch for 15 seconds. Keep your torso upright during this phase; don't let it bend forward. Relax, and repeat.

The Total Warm-Up Period

Combine the previous exercises with the basic skills activities in Step 1 to complete your warm-up. The total warm-up period is approximately a half hour, until your muscles feel warm and flexible and your basic stance on the skis is balanced and relaxed. You may repeat these exercises at the conclusion of your ski lesson or trail tour to prevent soreness or stiffness after exertion.

Step 1 Fundamental Skills

A *skill* is a simple move that usually focuses on one specific task. It is the ability to use your hands and feet with dexterity to perform a certain task. At the heart of cross-country skiing lie eight basic skills that compose the different maneuvers:

1. Gliding on one ski
2. Moving from ski to ski
3. Pushing off
4. Edging
5. Skidding
6. Steering
7. Poling
8. Gliding on two skis

Initial practice of the eight fundamental skills will make your skiing performance an easier and more enjoyable undertaking. These building blocks are simple tasks, easy to remember and learn. Isolating each skill lets your body memorize the movement quickly and begin to build a solid foundation for subsequent practice of maneuvers.

A *maneuver* requires a combination of skills to perform a certain function and is more complex as a result. Every maneuver combines several basic skills in a unique fashion. The more skills involved, the more complex the maneuver. Examples of maneuvers include the diagonal stride, double poling, skating, and wedge turns.

WHY ARE THE FUNDAMENTAL SKILLS SO IMPORTANT?

Each skill requires you to use your body in a precise manner to control the skis. How you use your body to maintain balance and rhythm in skiing will vary with each particular skill. All skills require a relaxed stance where your entire body acts as a shock absorber, able to absorb bumps and dips in terrain. This tension-free stance is also necessary to generate power efficiently to move across the snow, climb uphill, and descend hills with an ability to control speed.

Analyzing each maneuver in terms of its component skills also provides a better understanding of how the maneuver is executed. Skiers often perform the skills in a three- or four-step

sequence, which helps to break the move into identifiable parts. The skills enable you to better identify problems in your skiing, because an inability to perform a maneuver is usually caused by poor execution of a particular skill. Knowing the underlying skills provides you with a prescription to cure the problems.

HOW TO EXECUTE THE FUNDAMENTAL SKILLS

Practice the following eight skills, and ask a friend or ski instructor to provide you with feedback about your basic stance. In general, strive for a flexible, relaxed stance rather than rigid poses.

1. Gliding on One Ski

Gliding on one ski is an extremely important skill to develop, because the longer you glide on each ski, the easier you move across the snow. Initially, you may find yourself shuffling along the snow, unsure of your one-legged balance. But improving this skill is the key to developing more fluid and faster advanced skiing.

Stand flat-footed on one ski, and move your weight completely over it. Line up your nose, knee, and toe to prevent tipping from side to side. Bend your leg at the knee and ankle to settle your weight between the ball and heel of your foot. Again, the foot remains flat on the ski without any heel lift.

An important consideration is your hip position (see Figure 1.1). Keep your hips forward over your feet, rather than lagging behind them, to ride the ski in a balanced fashion. You can test how far to move your hips forward by bending forward from the ankle until you automatically take a step forward with the other leg to prevent falling. Just before this point is a good position for your hips.

Practice gliding on each leg on a very gentle incline, striving to remain on one ski for as long as possible. You may discover you are able to glide longer on one of your legs than on the other. Make sure that you strengthen the weaker leg with additional practice. Practice gliding on each ski until you can hold the other ski off the

Figure 1.1   Correct position for gliding on one ski.

snow without immediately putting it down again.

2. Moving From Ski to Ski

Moving from ski to ski involves a transfer of weight between skis. Strive to transfer your weight completely to move forward most efficiently. The goal is transferring weight crisply so that only one ski remains on the snow at a time. Otherwise, a shuffling action results that is stable but slow.

Move gently from ski to ski in a stationary position, and balance completely over each ski with your body aligned above it. Move slowly so you can feel and see a complete shift of your body from side to side (see Figure 1.2). If you tilt off the ski to the inside, then you've been too tentative and haven't moved your weight completely over the ski. Practice until you are able to stand flat-footed above each ski without rocking immediately back to the other ski.

Now practice moving from ski to ski more quickly, and lift one ski off the snow as soon as the other touches down. Keep only one ski on the snow at a time! Practice this crisp transfer until you can balance completely on each ski and hold the position briefly before returning to the other ski.

Begin to walk slowly across the snow, transferring weight crisply so that only one ski remains on the snow at a time. Dampen any excessive bobbing by stepping forward gently and quietly. Then slide each ski forward, again with only one ski on the snow at a time.

3. Pushing Off

Efficient pushoff is necessary to move forward without slipping on the skis. Push down against a flat foot to get good traction. The downward pressure sets the wax or patterned base into the snow, where it grips momentarily. This gripping provides a platform that enables you to move forward without slipping.

A leg that is flexed, particularly at the ankle, bends like a spring and allows you to extend forward after setting the wax. Effective pushoff is a matter of good timing. You push off each ski when your feet are side by side (see Figure 1.3). With your hips over your feet at this point, you can most effectively use your weight to get good traction and easily move forward. If you wait too long, your hips start to lag behind your feet, and your power diminishes.

Figure 1.2   Move from ski to ski by transferring your weight.

Figure 1.3   Correct pushing off position.

4. Edging

Edging helps the skis bite into the snow and prevents them from skidding excessively. The edge of the ski base digs into the snow, increasing resistance and slowing the ski. Edging is commonly used in turning to control speed and to help shape the turn, but it is also found in many skating moves.

You can edge your skis from a bent-leg stance by rolling your ankles and knees from side to side (see Figure 1.4). The skis roll from edge to edge as your knees swing above them. Loosen up your ankles by edging gently at first, and practice until you can swing your knees completely past each ski. This greater swing sets a harder edge.

Figure 1.5   Edging skis from a straight-leg stance.

Figure 1.4   Edging skis from a bent-leg stance.

This type of edging requires your body to be angulated along its length. Your legs bend in one direction, while your torso bends in another to keep your weight balanced over the skis.

Another method of edging comes from a straighter leg. Lean sideways or diagonally forward on a straight leg, and the tilt of your entire body sets the ski on edge (see Figure 1.5). This form of edging is often found in skating maneuvers, where the edged ski provides a firm platform from which to move forward. Balance on a straight leg, and lean your body diagonally forward. Watch the edge bite the snow as your weight moves forward.

5. Skidding

Skidding occurs when a flattened ski moves sideways across the snow. It is a common component of turns, where the skidding skis move sideways and forward down the hill. The flatter position of the skis lets them slip easily across the snow (see Figure 1.6).

Figure 1.6   Ski skidding aids turning.

A slightly flexed leg makes skidding easier to control. Stand comfortably on your skis with flexed legs, and push sideways against one ski with a flat foot. Equalize heel and toe pressure against the skidded ski so that it remains parallel to the one on which you are standing. If the ski turns, you are pushing more strongly with your toe or heel. To ensure good pressure against the ski, keep pushing until you develop a ridge of snow at the end of the skidding. The ridge should be parallel to your other ski.

Practice skidding with each leg. You may feel more comfortable skidding to one side if you have a dominant leg. Practice longer with the weaker leg, if necessary, until the ridge of snow at the end of the skidding is the same height as one developed on the other side.

6. Steering

Steering is a rotary motion of the feet and legs that turns the skis. To properly steer your skis, you must use your entire lower body. The crucial element is turning your foot with follow-through from the knee and hip. If you move just your knees, you will have trouble steering—you must engage your feet to pivot your skis against the snow.

Develop a feel for the subtlety of steering by pressing your ski tip against an immovable object, such as a ski pole planted between your skis. You should feel your big toe pressing against your boot. Now place the ski against the snow, and with your foot flat on the ski, press the tip against the pole again to turn the ski (see Figure 1.7). Then practice the rotary motion without a pole until you smoothly steer the ski into position.

Figure 1.7 Practice steering by pressing your tip into a planted ski pole.

Cross-country skiers, with their free heels, are wise to focus on their toes to steer. Your toes are closer to the binding than your heels and can better direct the skis.

7. Poling

There are two basic types of poling in cross-country skiing: alternate and double. In alternate poling, the arms swing independently of each other, as in the natural arm swing of walking or striding forward. In double poling, the arms push simultaneously against the poles.

Skiers commonly use these two types of poling to develop momentum. Alternate poling develops more consistent momentum, because one arm applies power while the other arm is returning to the plant position. Double poling, with its simultaneous arm action, provides a concentrated burst of power.

Alternate Poling

Alternate poling involves a backward pendular swing of the arm from the shoulder (see Figure 1.8). The arm is comfortably straight without being rigid, and it follows an arc when it swings. Extend your arm comfortably forward, no higher than shoulder level, and swing downward and past your body until your arm is extended fully rearward. Hold the pole gently but firmly enough to angle the shaft backward during this swing, and let your hand release the pole at the farthest point of rearward extension. This action completes the swing and relaxes your hand so the pole extends backward instead of toward the sky. Simultaneously, your other arm executes a forward pendular swing.

Figure 1.8 Use a backward pendular swing for alternate poling.

The pendular swing must be aligned with your ski to be effective. Your hand should not cross over the ski at any point, because this will cause excessive rotation of your torso that can unbalance you. Swing your arm forward until it aligns parallel to the ski. Also remember to extend each arm behind your body fully and lift it until you feel resistance.

Double Poling

Double poling involves swinging the arms simultaneously and actively using the larger, stronger torso muscles to provide additional power. Extend your arms comfortably forward to plant the poles, and bend at the waist to drop your torso's weight onto the poles (see Figure 1.9). Greater power results from involving the heavy torso than from using the smaller, weaker arm muscles. Extend your arms rearward, past your legs, and let your hands momentarily release the poles at fullest extension. Again, this action lets the poles extend backward; a tight, tense grasp would extend the poles upward.

Figure 1.9 Swing both arms simultaneously for double poling.

The up-and-down compression of the upper body is extremely important to provide good power. Bend over deeply, and come up completely to get the most power from this action. A slight flex at the knees, without bending the knees, eliminates lower back strain during the compression.

Although double poling can be used alone, it is also a part of many different ski maneuvers, particularly freestyle moves. The arm position is often varied to suit the particular move. The dynamics of these changes are discussed later in this book.

8. Gliding on Two Skis

Gliding on two skis is an important skill for handling any incline, gentle or steep. This secure position (see Figure 1.10) with the feet side by side provides great sideways stability. Beginning skiers appreciate the ability it gives them to ''ride out'' uneven terrain and snow conditions.

Figure 1.10 Correct position for gliding on two skis.

The basic stance requires flexed, active legs and an upright, quiet torso with no bend at the waist. Hands remain low in front of the body to lead the way, comfortably grasping the poles. Fight the tendency to focus on the ski tips! Look beyond your skis to the trail to anticipate the terrain ahead.

Stand with your feet shoulder-width apart; the wider stance supports your heavy shoulders and avoids the teetering that comes from a narrower base. Bend your legs at the knees and ankles, keeping the joints loose and flexible to absorb changes in terrain. The ankle flex is most important, because this action settles your weight between the balls and heels of the feet while preventing the ski tips from chattering on the snow. Maintain a flat-footed stance overall without lifting your heels off the skis. Avoid bending only at the knees; such a squatty position can send your weight toward your heels and make you fall backward.

Tilting your pelvis will help keep your back slightly rounded and reduce the lower back strain that can result from arching. It also positions your spine favorably for moving to many other skiing stances. This athletic, ready-for-anything stance is common to many sports, because it provides a stable ''platform'' for moving from one maneuver to another.

HOW TO FALL AND GET UP SAFELY

Falling is an inevitable part of Nordic skiing. It may occur spontaneously during your warm-up period, and should not be feared. When you begin to lose your balance, remember "to get small in a ball." Tucking in your arms and curling up your body lessens the possibility of injury and cushions the fall.

If your poles and skis become tangled when you fall, roll over on your back and untangle your gear. While on your back, orient your skis so they are parallel, lying on the snow. Crawl forward and get onto your knees. Then, slide a ski forward and stand up. You can use your poles for support as you rise, but don't try to push yourself up with your poles. Your skis can shoot forward, and you will fall again. In deep snow, you can create an X with your poles next to your ski tip and push off this platform before standing.

The same procedure will work later in your development. If you fall on a hill remember to swing your skis to the downhill side of your body and place them perpendicular to the fall line. Then push off the snow on the uphill side of your skis to stand up.

HOW TO PRACTICE THE FUNDAMENTAL SKILLS

After completing the warm-up exercises in "Preparing Your Body for Success," begin your practice of the eight basic skills. The practice drills proceed from easier to more difficult skills. The total practice period for warm-up plus basic drills is approximately a half hour. This will prepare you for ski maneuvers.

The best place to practice is on flat, groomed terrain that is free of tracks. Deep, unpacked snow or an icy surface can make the drills difficult. The best site is often a groomed practice area at a cross-country ski center.

Some of the drills are designed for in-place practice; others ask you to move on flat terrain. Choose at least two drills for each skill. For increased comfort, begin with an in-place exercise and finish with a moving exercise. If a particular skill feels uncomfortable, select another drill for additional practice of that skill.

Don't use your poles for most of the drills. Let your body learn how to balance effectively on the skis without them. Use the poles only for the poling and gliding on two skis drills at the end of the practice period, just prior to beginning the ski maneuvers.

Gliding on One Ski Drills (Basic Skill #1)

1. *Stork Stance*: Stand on one ski, and center your weight directly over the ski. Bend your leg at the knee and ankle to lower your body slightly and improve balance. Look up rather than down at the ski. Hold the position as long as possible.

   Close your eyes and repeat the exercise. Focus on your foot, which should be flat on the ski. Feel your weight settle between your toes and heel for good balance.

   Repeat the drill with the other leg.

2. *One-Ski Scooters*: Prepare to ski approximately 25 yards toward a landmark in the distance (a building, tree, trail sign, etc.). Remove one ski, and stand on the other ski as if you were balancing on a scooter. Use the free foot to help push you toward your landmark. Look at the landmark while you glide on the ski (rather than looking down at the ground) to keep your

Figure 1.11   One-ski scooters.

body erect and balanced better over the gliding foot (see Figure 1.11).

Repeat the exercise with the other leg. If you notice that your balance is better on one leg than on the other, repeat the exercise with the weaker leg.

3. *Tandem Scooters*: Link arms with another skier who is also using only one ski. Push off and glide in a synchronized fashion. Holding onto another person helps you maintain your balance. Strive for a smooth, balanced glide. Experiment with different ski combinations: each skier gliding on the same foot, pushing with inside feet, gliding on inside feet. You'll find that your ability to glide smoothly and farther will increase quickly.

4. *Longest One-Ski Glide*: Use a very gentle incline, where the grade allows you to glide comfortably on one ski. Mark a starting line at the top. Push off and glide as far as possible on one ski. Mark the ending point (with, say, a twig, hat, or mitten). Descend again with the same gliding leg, trying to pass your first end point.

Repeat the exercise with the other leg. Compare the distances with each leg, and repeat the exercise with the weaker leg.

5. *Two-Step Glide*: Wear both skis for this drill. Flat terrain is best, to enhance balance. Stride along the snow with an even tempo, and begin to count your strides. Begin to glide longer with every third stride, riding the gliding ski as long as possible before you take the next step. Use this cadence: stride-stride-glide, stride-stride-glide. The two-step glide sequence ensures that you switch gliding legs.

Moving From Ski to Ski Drills (Basic Skill #2)

1. *Hop Drill*: Hop quickly in place from ski to ski with only one ski on the snow at a time. Begin with a moderate tempo, and then change the pace from fast to slow. Use your arms at first, to aid balance, but strive to keep them low and quiet at the end of the drill.

2. *Hop-Hold Drill*: Continue to hop from ski to ski, but gradually slow your weight transfer. As the pace slows, you'll have to center your weight longer over each ski. Finish by balancing as long as possible on

each ski. Keep the foot flat upon the ski. A bent leg also helps to lower your center of gravity and improve balance. Strive to keep your hands low and quiet at the end of the drill.

3. *Toe-Knee-Nose Shifts*: Stride slowly across the snow, shifting your weight completely from ski to ski as you stride. Align your knees and nose over the toes to center your weight on the ski. As you move to the other ski, align your toes, knee, and nose again. Look just past the ski tips while you move between the skis, and you'll see your body shift from side to side.

Pushing Off Drills (Basic Skill #3)

1. *Leg Springs*: Without skis, hop in place, and exaggerate the flex in your legs. Bend sharply at the ankle to increase the height of your hop as you spring upward. Now hop from ski to ski with exaggerated pushoff. Keep your landing leg flexible. Vary the leg flex from shallow to deep, and feel the pushoff increase in power.

2. *Push-Overs*: Take off your skis, and lay your ski poles (or a rope) in a straight line. Leap diagonally forward over the line in a relaxed fashion, standing on only one foot at a time. Hold each position until you are balanced quietly on your foot.

Repeat the exercise with skis, but flex your leg deeply to push off strongly (see Figure 1.12). Extend the width of your path by leaping farther sideways. You'll have to work harder to stand flat-footed

Figure 1.12 Push-overs.

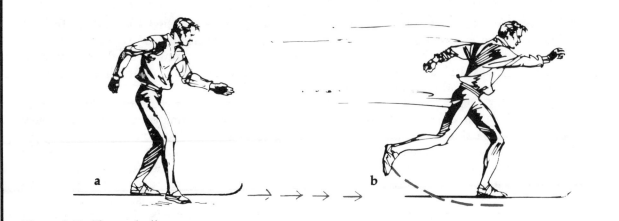

Figure 1.13 The pushoff zone.

and balanced at the end of each leap. Repeat the exercise until you can no longer widen your path. This exercise is excellent preparation for skating.

3. *One-Ski Leaps*: Remove one ski for this exercise, and use your free leg as the pushoff leg. Bend your free leg deeply, and leap onto your ski to ride out the glide (see Figure 1.13, a and b). Bring your hips up and forward to stay centered over the ski. Straighten your gliding leg, but keep it slightly flexed so you can ride the ski smoothly.

Repeat the exercise with the other leg.

4. *The Pushoff Zone*: Prepare to scooter along the snow on one ski. Push off when your free foot is beside or slightly in front of your gliding foot. Treat this area around the gliding foot as a transition zone. It's the most effective place to push off, because your weight is over or slightly forward of your feet, where traction is the best.

Edging Drills
(Basic Skill #4)

1. *Leg Angulation*: Stand flat-footed on your skis with your feet beneath your hips. This position creates a wide stance. Swing your knees from side to side, and watch your skis roll from edge to edge. Vary your knee swing from slight to vigorous, and watch the edging change from gentle to strong. This exercise shows how you can edge your skis with an angulated leg.

2. *Giant Steps*: Take a giant step sideways, and watch how your ski naturally edges against the snow as you move away from

it. Keep changing direction with more giant steps, and feel how securely you can step off the edges of the skis.

3. *Catch-Your-Partner Drill*: Stand 5 feet from another skier, with your skis parallel. Begin to step sideways in the same direction, keeping the skis parallel. Increase the speed of the sidestepping, and try to tag your partner. Change direction when you've tagged; now the other skier chases you. As your sidestepping speeds up, you'll begin to take larger steps and edge your skis strongly to move sideways quickly.

4. *Tandem Tug-of-War*: Stand facing a partner, and hold your partner's hand that is closest to you. Use a wide ski stance for a secure platform, and try to gently pull each other off balance (see Figure 1.14). You'll naturally dig into the snow with your ski edges to get leverage against your partner.

Figure 1.14 Tandem tug-of-war.

Skidding Drills
(Basic Skill #5)

1. *Pushaways*: Stand upright in a wide stance with skis parallel. Push sideways against the snow with one ski. Use enough pressure against the ski to uniformly push the snow into a straight ridge. Keep your foot flat on the ski to equalize the pressure along the entire ski length, and use a bent leg for a more powerful push. Perform enough pushaways to develop a distinct snow ridge that is uniform in height. You may have to push harder with your toe or heel to create a uniform ridge. Repeat the exercise with the other leg.

2. *Waltzing*: Begin with a wide stance. Push away snow with one ski and then stand on the ski. Change direction, and push away snow with the other ski and stand on the ski. As you push back and forth, you will develop a waltzing rhythm. Waltz until you create two ridges of snow outside your skis.

3. *Parallel Hops*: From a parallel stance, hop gently from side to side. Keep your legs flexed and relaxed. Then let the skis drift across the snow without lifting off it. Widen the distance between hops, and let the skis skid to a stop with each hop. Repeat until the skis smoothly drift across the snow without snagging.

Steering Drills
(Basic Skill #6)

1. *Ski Pole Press*: Plant a ski pole between your ski tips, lift one ski, and press the ski against the pole (review Figure 1.7). Feel how your big toe presses against the inside of your boot. Now use your entire leg for additional pressure, and watch your knee move inward toward the pole. This rotary action of the leg is what makes the ski turn. Repeat with the other leg.

   Plant the pole on the outside of one ski. Press the ski against the pole, using the outside of the foot. Now the little toe applies pressure against the boot. Repeat with the other leg.

2. *Wedge Jumps*: From a parallel stance, jump into the air and turn your feet inward. When you land on the snow, your ski tips will be closer together and the tails farther apart. The skis form a wedge or pie shape.

Land on relaxed legs that remain bent at the knees and ankles. Practice jumping into this wedge position until your tips consistently land about 6 inches apart.

3. *Snow Brushes*: Stand with your skis shoulder-width apart. Push sideways with one ski, and rotate your foot at the same time. You'll brush the snow with an angled ski to create a wedge-shaped depression in the snow (see Figure 1.15, a and b). Press your big toe against the side of the boot so you get equal pressure against the tip and the tail of the ski. Also, bend your leg at the knee and ankle to apply force against the ski. Brush several times to create an obvious depression in the snow.

   Repeat with the other leg.

a

b

Figure 1.15 Snow brushes, preparation (a), execution (b).

4. *Steered Wedges*: Stand with your skis shoulder-width apart. Simultaneously press flat-footed against each ski to move them farther apart, and rotate your toes

inward so the tips are close together. Increase the flex in your legs to drop your weight downward against the skis.

If you have difficulty pressing the skis apart, then widen your stance. If you have difficulty steering the skis into position, check to make sure your legs are flexed and your feet are flat against the skis to apply equal pressure to the entire ski length.

5. *Star Turns*: Plant a pole near the tips of your skis. Turn around the pole by keeping your tips near it and moving your tails to step sideways. You'll step from one wedge position to another as you move around the pole. Small steps work best to control your skis and to avoid stepping on the tips (see Figure 1.16).

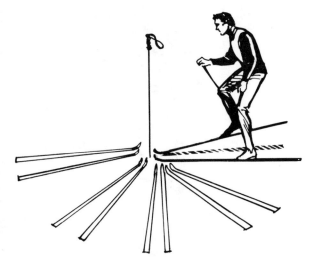

Figure 1.16   Star turns.

Now plant the pole at the tails of your skis. Step around the pole by keeping your tails near it and moving your tips to step sideways. Again, small steps work best to avoid stepping on the tails of your skis.

Poling Drills
(Basic Skill #7)

1. *Alternate Poling*: Hold your pole grips loosely and prepare to swing your arms without planting the poles. Extend one arm comfortably forward to shoulder height with a slight bend at the elbows.

Extend the other arm backward until you feel resistance in your shoulder. Swing the arm in front of you downward and past the thigh while simultaneously swinging the opposite arm forward. Repeat until the alternating arm swing feels comfortable.

2. *Double Poling*: Hold your pole grips loosely and prepare to swing your arms without planting the poles. Extend both arms comfortably forward to shoulder height with a slight bend at the elbow. Swing your arms downward, past the thighs, and bend fully at the waist until your back is parallel to the ground. Swing your hands behind your body until you feel resistance in your shoulders. Now swing your arms forward and begin to raise your torso. As your hands reach shoulder height, your body should be upright and your hips forward. Repeat until your torso moves up and down in unison with the forward and backward arm swing.

Gliding on Two Skis Drills
(Basic Skill #8)

1. *Shuffle and Glide*: Shuffle on flat terrain until you move quickly enough to glide on your skis for 2 to 3 feet. Flex your ankles and knees to maintain your balance. Shuffle more quickly until you can change to gliding without wobbling on your skis.

2. *Gentle Descents*: Practice the basic stance while stationary, letting your shins press forward against your boots until your knees are partially over your feet. Then descend a gentle incline with your joints flexing to handle any changes in terrain. Practice sliding until you have eliminated wobbling and feel comfortable with your balance.

SUMMARY

This initial skills practice orients you to your ski equipment, awakens your body to the underlying components of all cross-country maneuvers, and relaxes you for subsequent practice. Once you have developed increased stability and comfort on your skis, you are ready to practice the various maneuvers.

Step 2 Diagonal Striding

Skiers use the diagonal stride to begin to move along the tracks on flat terrain. It is the most common maneuver in classical skiing and an elegant, powerful image that inspires many new skiers. The diagonal stride can be performed at first in a slower, touring mode to improve one's balance and later in an aggressive recreational or racing mode to increase one's speed. Because it is the most commonly used move, the diagonal stride is the place to begin.

"Diagonal" refers here to the opposite action of the arms and legs that occurs naturally when you walk or run. A diagonal line is also evident in the form of a cross-country skier who is leaning forward and gliding fully on each leg. This coordination of arms and legs should be a natural process, and too much thinking—"Right leg and left arm forward at the same time"—can interfere with your learning. Think of it as a natural extension of a gentle jog, and you will capture the essence of a relaxed diagonal stride.

WHY IS THE DIAGONAL STRIDE IMPORTANT?

The diagonal stride is the easiest way for a skier to move across the snow. This stride's similarity to walking and jogging provides you with a familiar series of actions that help you quickly develop good rhythm and balance. This versatile maneuver also works well in both groomed and ungroomed snow conditions, so it allows you to ski successfully in many different outdoor environments.

The diagonal stride also provides a secure way for you to become accustomed to your ski equipment. You may at first be disconcerted to have only your toes attached to the skis and your heels free to lift from them, but the free heels enable you to explore a wealth of terrain—you can ski across flat ground as well as stride efficiently uphill with this maneuver.

HOW TO EXECUTE THE DIAGONAL STRIDE

The best strategy is to start by walking on your skis to discover the naturally correct timing of your arms and legs. Then jog and stride gently to reinforce good timing. Effective timing of the arms and legs is crucial to a well-executed diagonal stride. The initial walking and jogging on your skis captures the timing effectively and sets the stage for you to achieve the ultimate goal—gliding on each ski as you stride forward.

If you have difficulty coordinating the arm-leg movement, practice without your poles, which you might be using to help yourself balance. Reliance on poles often interrupts the natural rhythm of the maneuver by slowing the arms and creating poor timing. Walk, jog, and stride gently to recapture the coordination. A gentle incline, where you pump your arms naturally to stride uphill with shorter steps, also helps to rediscover proper timing.

Striving for a long glide at the outset can undermine your learning, because your one-legged balance may need improvement. Return to the one-legged gliding exercises in Step 1 if you have difficulty balancing on one ski at a time. Don't overlook this practice, because one-legged balance is the most important skill in more dynamic diagonal striding (see Figure 2.1a).

Once your timing is coordinated, focus next on transferring your weight crisply from ski to ski. This style of short-step skiing reinforces good timing and encourages you to stride on one ski at a time—for only a short time! It helps you maintain your balance, because your body remains over your feet rather than behind them, and your legs remain flexed at the ankle and knee (see Figure 2.1, b and c). Try to increase the glide slightly during this phase to begin to move from a shorter jogging/trotting tempo into a longer striding/gliding tempo. Strive for only a few inches of extra glide, instead of a foot, to maintain good timing!

Moving beyond this point can be counterproductive until you improve your ability to glide comfortably on one ski at a time. The most important focus is preserving good timing and balance before attempting to glide more aggressively.

Too many people strive for that extended pose associated with the diagonal stride by lifting the rear leg off the snow. Extension of the leg is actually a natural reaction to pushing off the snow forcefully and moving forward. Focus on pushing off with each foot at the proper time—when your feet are side by side and your body is over the feet. A well-timed pushoff provides the necessary traction and power to move forward efficiently. Do not deliberately lift your rear leg, because it can develop a weak pushoff that occurs too late.

Figure 2.1 Keys to Success: Diagonal Striding

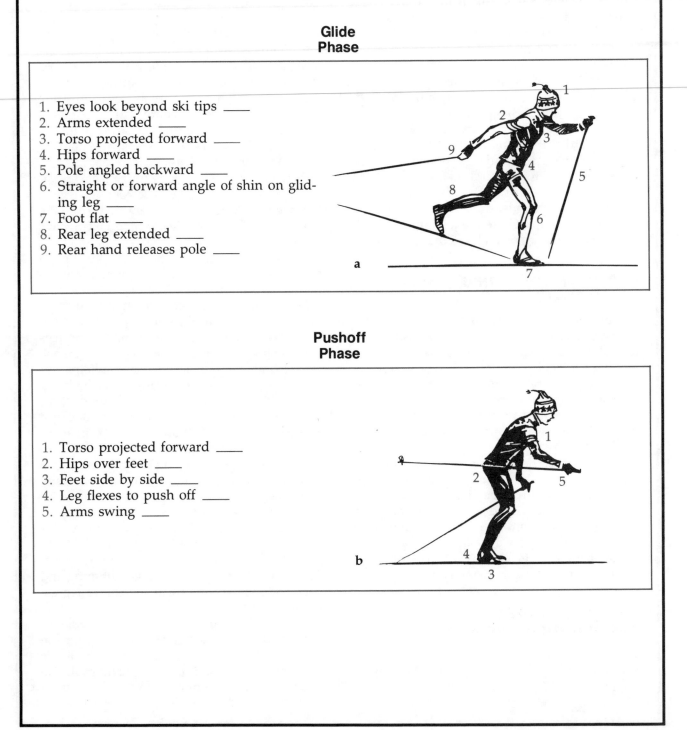

Glide Phase

1. Eyes look beyond ski tips ____
2. Arms extended ____
3. Torso projected forward ____
4. Hips forward ____
5. Pole angled backward ____
6. Straight or forward angle of shin on gliding leg ____
7. Foot flat ____
8. Rear leg extended ____
9. Rear hand releases pole ____

Pushoff Phase

1. Torso projected forward ____
2. Hips over feet ____
3. Feet side by side ____
4. Leg flexes to push off ____
5. Arms swing ____

**New Glide
Phase**

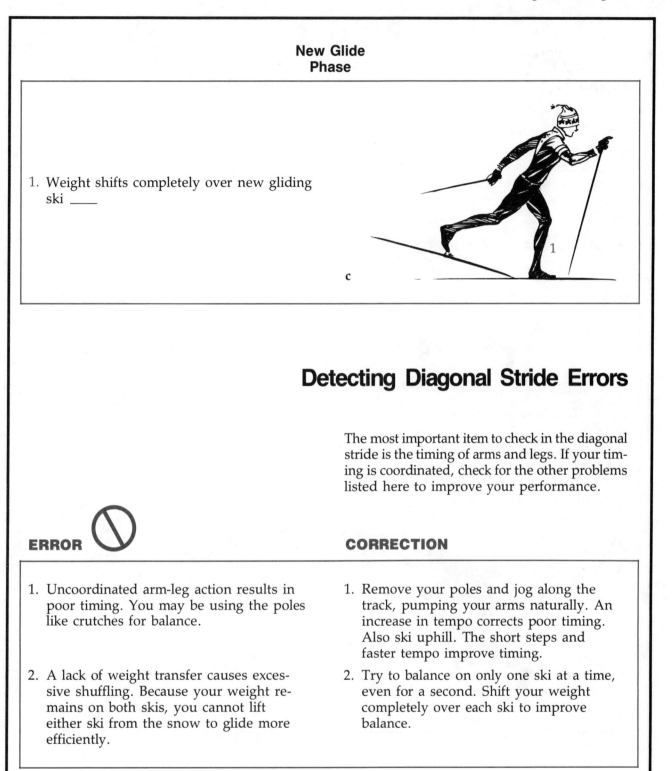

1. Weight shifts completely over new gliding
ski ____

Detecting Diagonal Stride Errors

The most important item to check in the diagonal stride is the timing of arms and legs. If your timing is coordinated, check for the other problems listed here to improve your performance.

ERROR

CORRECTION

1. Uncoordinated arm-leg action results in poor timing. You may be using the poles like crutches for balance.

1. Remove your poles and jog along the track, pumping your arms naturally. An increase in tempo corrects poor timing. Also ski uphill. The short steps and faster tempo improve timing.

2. A lack of weight transfer causes excessive shuffling. Because your weight remains on both skis, you cannot lift either ski from the snow to glide more efficiently.

2. Try to balance on only one ski at a time, even for a second. Shift your weight completely over each ski to improve balance.

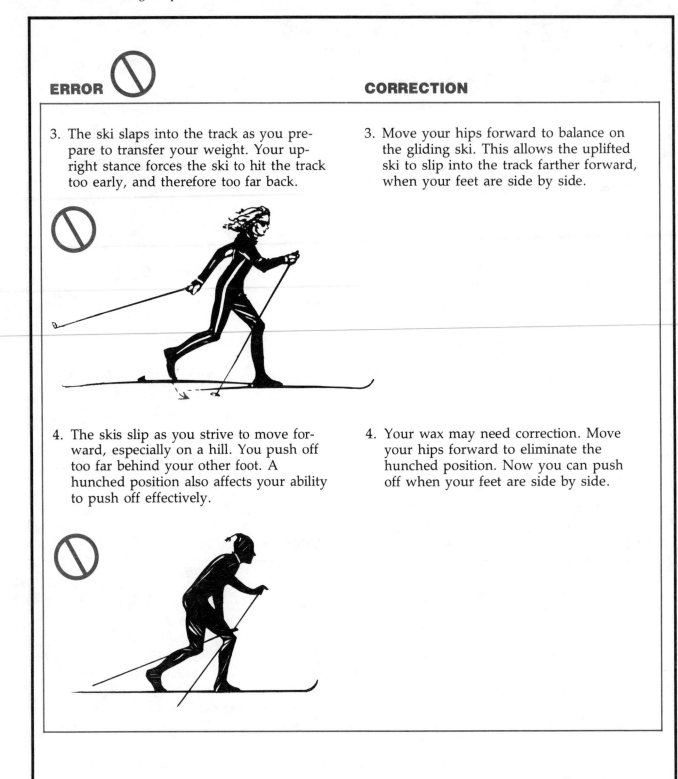

ERROR

CORRECTION

3. The ski slaps into the track as you prepare to transfer your weight. Your upright stance forces the ski to hit the track too early, and therefore too far back.

3. Move your hips forward to balance on the gliding ski. This allows the uplifted ski to slip into the track farther forward, when your feet are side by side.

4. The skis slip as you strive to move forward, especially on a hill. You push off too far behind your other foot. A hunched position also affects your ability to push off effectively.

4. Your wax may need correction. Move your hips forward to eliminate the hunched position. Now you can push off when your feet are side by side.

Diagonal Stride Drills

1. No-Poles Drill

Eliminating the poles helps develop good balance, because you cannot use the poles as crutches. It encourages proper use of your legs and positioning of your torso to maintain balance. Use a

50-yard stretch of tracks that are relatively straight and flat. A trail with curves around corners can interfere initially with your ability to develop consistent rhythm.

Walk down the tracks, swinging your arms naturally as if you were walking down a road. As your left arm moves forward, so should the right leg. Let your skis slide in the tracks without lifting from the snow. Return along your practice tracks to your beginning point. Continue to walk along this course until you can walk 50 yards without wobbling.

Now shuffle down the track, swinging your arms backward and forward more aggressively. Let your skis slide along in the tracks without lifting and stepping. A quicker tempo will result, and you'll cover the distance faster and more naturally. Continue to shuffle until you can shuffle 50 yards without a pause or glitch in your rhythm.

Success Goal = 100 yards of balanced walking and shuffling

    a. 50 yards walking (without poles)

    b. 50 yards shuffling (without poles)

Your Score =

    a. (#) _____ yards of balanced walking

    b. (#) _____ yards of balanced shuffling

2. Arm Swings Drill

Continue to use the same 50-yard practice course to monitor the path of your arm swing. The goal is swinging your arms efficiently so that your hands stay to the outside of the tracks and aligned with them. Your hands should not move inward and cross over the tracks. If your hand crosses over the tracks in front of your body, you are swinging the arm around rather than straight forward and back. If you cross over with your poling, you will probably fall to the outside of your skis, because your overly active torso has rotated around and your body is no longer centered over the skis.

Use your poles to help orient your arms to the proper path. Hold the poles at midshaft, swinging them naturally as you shuffle down the track again. Align the poles with the track, so they swing backward and forward without crossing over your skis. The poles provide a very clear indicator of any crossover. Practice until you can swing your arms efficiently for 50 yards without crossing over.

Continue to hold the poles at midshaft for the next phase. Now swing the poles and point the pole end down the track at full forward extension. The pole should stay relatively horizontal to the ground at this point. Pointing the pole down the track orients your body and momentum down the track, rather than sending your momentum upward toward the sky.

Success Goal = 100 yards of efficient arm swings

    a. 50 yards of arm swings with no crossover

    b. 50 yards of arm swings with pole pointed down the track

Your Score =

    a. (#) _____ yards of efficient arm swings with no crossover

    b. (#) _____ yards of efficient arm swings with pole pointed down the track

3. Shuffle-Jog-Stride Drill

Use a 50-yard set of straight tracks on flat terrain. Deep, well-formed tracks will direct your skis easily; the skis may move from side to side in shallow tracks when you stride more actively.

Begin by shuffling along the tracks in your practice area. Let your arms pump rhythmically to establish good coordination between your arms and legs. Repeat the shuffling until you can ski 25 yards without any pauses in your rhythm that are caused by loss of balance.

Quicken the tempo and jog down the tracks. Your arms begin to move more quickly and pump harder. Jogging keeps you moving quickly from ski to ski and improves balance. Repeat the jogging until you can ski the practice course one way (50 yards) without any disruptions in the rhythm.

Jogging on skis is a temporary stage that reinforces the proper coordination of arms and legs. Because jogging can encourage too much up-and-down bobbing and consumes a lot of energy, the next step is smoothing the jogging into a short stride.

Let your skis glide forward slightly with each step. Strive for a forward movement of several inches rather than a foot, because the short step requires that you keep your body centered over the gliding ski for a shorter period of time. It allows you to keep your body forward over your feet to ride the forward ski comfortably. If you become unbalanced, shorten your step-stride slightly until you can ski 50 yards smoothly.

Success Goal = Shuffling, jogging, and striding with consistent rhythm

    a. 25 yards of balanced, rhythmic shuffling

    b. 50 yards of continuous, balanced jogging

    c. 50 yards of continuous, balanced, short-step striding

Your Score =

    a. (#) _____ yards of rhythmic shuffling

    b. (#) _____ yards of rhythmic jogging

    c. (#) _____ yards of rhythmic short-step striding

4. Gentle Poling Drill

Proper poling can enhance your striding, once you have your arms and legs well coordinated. First let your poles hang loosely. Wear the straps like bracelets and refrain from grabbing the grips. Use short strides to ski along a 50-yard practice course, swinging your arms without planting the poles. Pretend you do not have any poles, and swing your arms naturally. It's OK if your poles swing erratically as they drag on the snow—the focus here is reestablishing good arm-leg coordination. Ask a ski professional to check that your timing is proper.

In the next phase, continue to wear the pole straps like bracelets and prepare to apply very gentle pressure against the pole straps. Swing your arm forward to the plant position; your arm will be bent slightly, the hand at about shoulder height, and the pole angled backward with the pole tip at or behind your foot (depending upon the length of your poles). Do not lift the pole tip off the snow; you will have lifted your hand too high at the plant position and moved the pole into a vertical position. Ask a ski professional or another skier to watch whether the pole tip lifts off the snow.

Apply pressure against the strap with the palm of your hand as you move the hand downward and backward behind your body to complete the pendular swing. Repeat the same sequence when the other hand swings forward for the pole plant. This gentle pressure helps you to retain good timing. Gripping the pole strongly at the outset can create tension in your body that undermines your rhythm. Ski 50 yards with gentle pressure against the wrist straps.

Next, hold the pole between your thumb and forefinger, which allows you to better control the pole swing. Again, hand pressure against the pole is minimal. Extend your arm backward behind your body, and at the end of the arm swing, point your hand backward (not downward) at the tracks you have just skied. Ski 50 yards with a thumb-forefinger grasp during the pole plants.

Finally, hold the poles loosely with your entire hand, and pole gently as you stride down the tracks. Release the pole at the point of farthest rearward extension of the arm. The pole grip remains loosely clasped by the thumb and forefinger, while the remaining fingers loosen and point directly backward. Ski 50 yards with these gentle pole plants.

Learning how to ski can be a tense experience as you concentrate intently upon improvements. If tension in your body is undermining your skiing, you relax by loosening your hand grip. This simple act can improve the fluidity of your skiing immensely. If you lose arm-leg coordination at any point, return to swinging your arms without planting the poles.

Success Goal = 200 yards striding and poling with correct arm-leg timing

  a. 50 yards with ''bracelet'' pole pushing

  b. 50 yards with ''strap-pressure'' pole pushing

  c. 50 yards with ''thumb-forefinger'' pole pushing

  d. 50 yards with gentle pole pushing

Your Score =

  a. (#) ____ yards of ''bracelet'' pole pushing

  b. (#) ____ yards of ''strap-pressure'' pole pushing

  c. (#) ____ yards of ''thumb-forefinger'' pole pushing

  d. (#) ____ yards of gentle pole pushing

5. Stride-Stride-Glide Drill

This drill is a more advanced step that seeks to improve one-ski balance. The sequence requires that you follow this sequence: stride, stride, and then glide longer on the third stride. Ride this gliding ski until your speed diminishes. Then repeat the stride-stride-glide sequence, gliding now on the opposite leg.

It is natural to wobble slightly on the gliding stride until your balance improves. Center your body over the gliding foot; you must completely move your weight over the ski to be centered. Using short strides with a quicker tempo will help you maintain your balance.

Continue this practice until you have been able to ride the gliding ski 10 times without losing your balance.

Success Goal = 10 glides without losing balance

Your Score = (#) ____ balanced glides

Diagonal Stride
Keys to Success Checklist

Ask a trained observer—an instructor, a coach, or a knowledgeable skier—to check your arm-leg coordination during the diagonal stride. The observer should use the checklist in Figure 2.1 to evaluate the forward projection of your torso, angled poles, pendulum swing of your arms, and crisp weight transfer.

Step 3 Double Poling

Double poling is a good alternative to the diagonal stride for moving across flat terrain or a gentle downhill. This stable maneuver enables you to better handle the speed of faster snow conditions and slight hills, where momentum usually increases. It becomes difficult in slower, fresher snow when momentum is decreasing and poling alone cannot keep you moving.

Double poling uses synchronized arm swings enhanced by a bending of the torso. This compression of the upper body engages the powerful torso muscles to boost the power created by the arms. It is a simple move that can be easier to learn than the diagonal stride.

WHY IS DOUBLE POLING IMPORTANT?

Double poling provides greater lateral stability than the diagonal stride, because the feet remain side by side throughout the move. This sure-footed position lets you glide more comfortably across uneven terrain, particularly bumps and dips where balance is a problem. The maneuver also works effectively in gliding across uneven snow conditions, particularly irregular tracks and icy patches.

Double poling requires active bending of the torso to impart power to the arm swing. The use of the larger, stronger torso muscles increases the leverage you have against the poles. Because the move calls upon these new muscles, it provides your body with a welcome alternative to the diagonal stride. The deep waist bend stretches your lower back and relieves the fatigue that can result from striving to balance on each ski in the diagonal stride.

Because skating relies upon many forms of double poling for increased power, mastering basic double poling is an important step before learning to skate. It allows you to focus more completely upon the new leg movements involved in skating.

HOW TO DOUBLE POLE

The arms and body work together fluidly in the double pole without being rigidly locked together as one unit. The body rises and falls rhythmically, while the arms swing smoothly backward and forward.

Start from an upright stance with hips over feet and feet comfortably apart for secure balance. The feet stay just inside shoulder-width to create a solid platform. Keep your legs comfortably relaxed. Locking the knees puts too much strain on the back; flex them slightly. Overall, the legs bend very little during double poling; they provide a fulcrum around which the rest of the body moves.

Raise your hands to shoulder level to plant the poles at an angle to the snow (see Figure 3.1a). The longer your poles, the farther the pole tips extend behind your body, and the greater the angle of the poles against the snow. Extend your arms comfortably; some bend at the elbow works well at the outset to generate more power to get moving.

Begin to bend from the waist to bring your head toward the poles, and then push downward against the poles. The stomach muscles contract during this phase to begin the sequence. Swing your arms down past your shins and behind your body to complete the poling. Bend over completely until your back is parallel to the ground (see Figure 3.1b).

Extend your arms fully rearward until you feel resistance in your shoulders (see Figure 3.1c). Your torso begins to rise again during the follow-through. Recover the poles to return to the upright position from which you began. Your torso now gets to rest momentarily, before your arms begin double poling again.

For more aggressive poling, plant the poles ahead of your feet at a more vertical angle. Given the speed at which your feet are gliding forward, you actually end up pushing against an angled pole.

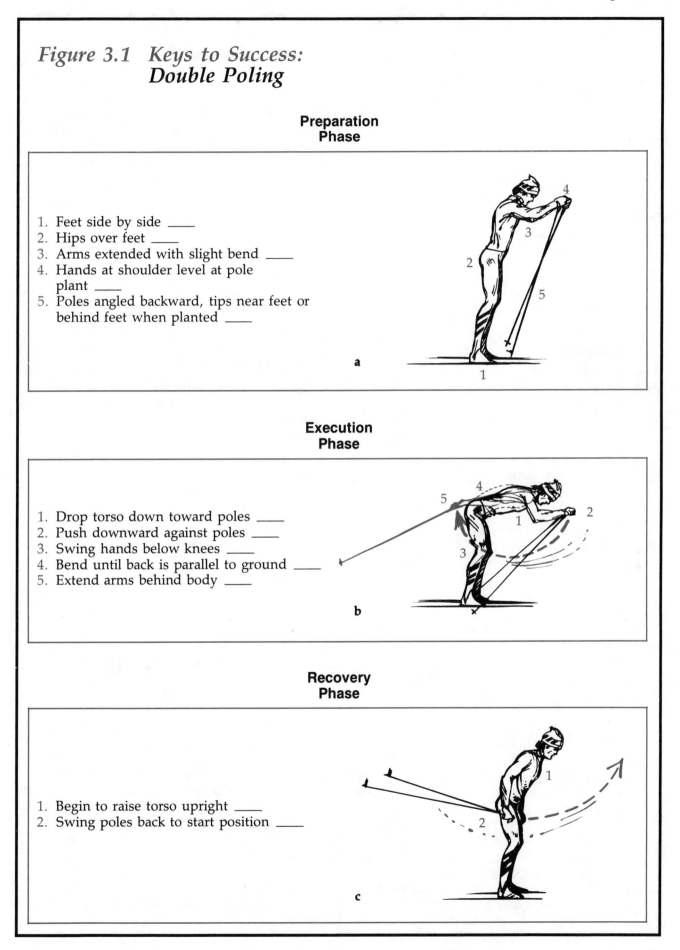

Figure 3.1 Keys to Success:
Double Poling

Preparation Phase

1. Feet side by side ____
2. Hips over feet ____
3. Arms extended with slight bend ____
4. Hands at shoulder level at pole plant ____
5. Poles angled backward, tips near feet or behind feet when planted ____

Execution Phase

1. Drop torso down toward poles ____
2. Push downward against poles ____
3. Swing hands below knees ____
4. Bend until back is parallel to ground ____
5. Extend arms behind body ____

Recovery Phase

1. Begin to raise torso upright ____
2. Swing poles back to start position ____

Detecting Double-Poling Errors

When you lack power or feel yourself straining through the double poling, you need to identify which part of your body is moving inefficiently. Common problems are identified in this section with suggestions for avoiding them.

ERROR 🚫

CORRECTION

ERROR	CORRECTION
1. The poles lift excessively above the snow before the pole plant.	1. During pole recovery, let the tips drag along the snow until your hands return to shoulder level to plant the poles.
2. The poles angle forward rather than backward before the pole plant.	2. End the pole recovery when the tips are near your feet rather than swinging them farther forward.
3. A lack of torso compression creates arm fatigue.	3. Raise your torso upright until your hips move forward, and bend it completely downward so your hands brush past your shins.
4. Your hips remain behind your feet and inhibit momentum.	4. In the upright position, bring your hips forward until the wrinkles leave your clothing. Bend forward from the ankles, and lean your body forward.
5. Your legs bend excessively, and you squat during poling.	5. Stiffen your legs, and then flex them slightly at the knee. Now bend over without bending your knees.

Double-Poling Drills

1. Mimetic Drill

Without planting your poles, practice the three different phases of double poling: preparation, execution, and recovery. Practice the sequence in a continuous motion with a focus on each individual phase.

Ask a friend to watch you practice and make sure you compress deeply until your back is parallel to the ground. Raise your torso completely and return to an upright position. Also ask the friend to check that you swing the poles behind your body completely.

Then repeat the practice with your eyes closed, which helps to focus your attention upon your body. First concentrate upon your stomach muscles, contracting them as you bend over and extending them as you return to the upright stance. Then follow the swing of your arms, brushing your hands past your shins and feeling the resistance in your shoulders that results from complete follow-through. Recover the poles by the same path.

Success Goal = 20 total sequences

   a. 10 with eyes open

   b. 10 with eyes closed

Your Score =

   a. (#) _____ sequences with eyes open

   b. (#) _____ sequences with eyes closed

2. *Synchronized Poling Drill*

Select an area where double tracks are set on flat terrain or a very gentle, slow downhill. Use double poling to ski beside a partner, and synchronize the rhythm of your poling. Then focus on each phase of the sequence, coaching each other if improvements are necessary.

First check your pole plant and determine whether your hands are approximately at shoulder level with the poles angled backward. Then compress your torso deeply to get more power when poling, trying to drop your back parallel to the ground. Finally, extend the poles fully behind, until you feel the poles "shoot" backward.

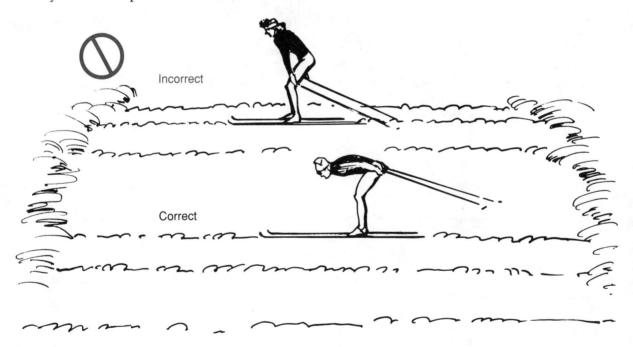

Incorrect

Correct

Success Goal = 30 total double-poling sequences with correct form

   a. 10 sequences to check the hand/pole position

   b. 10 sequences to check torso compression

   c. 10 sequences to check arm extension

Your Score =

   a. (#) _____ sequences with correct hand/pole position

   b. (#) _____ sequences with correct torso compression

   c. (#) _____ sequences with correct arm extension

3. Point A to Point B Drill

Establish a starting point (A) and a finishing point (B) along 50 yards of level tracks. Warm up by double-poling down and back on the track to become comfortable with any dips in the terrain. Then double-pole casually down the track and count the number of poling sequences (each time the poles are planted) between the two points.

   Double-pole along the course again, and try to reduce the number of double-pole sequences to improve your efficiency. Experiment with bending your upper body deeper or extending your poling to reduce your total number. Double-pole along the course until you can no longer improve your score.

Success Goal = Reduce the total number of double-poling sequences in each successive run until you cannot eliminate any more

Your Score =

   a. (#) _____ double-poling sequences in first run

   b. (#) _____ double-poling sequences in second run

   c. (#) _____ double-poling sequences in third run

   d. (#) _____ double-poling sequences in final run

4. Double-Pole Glide Drill

Use a set of tracks on flat terrain, and establish a starting line where you begin the sequence. Double-pole five times, and mark your ending point (*e.g.*, with a hat or twig). Return to the starting line, and repeat the sequence, striving to beat your original mark. Use deeper torso compressions or more powerful poling to extend your record down the track. See how far you can go to establish a "personal best."

Avoiding a quick tempo is helpful. Longer, rhythmic poling allows you to take advantage of the gliding, and it provides restful pauses.

Success Goal = Establishing a personal best along the track

Your Score =

   a. (#) _____ total yards traveled in first run

   b. (#) _____ total yards traveled in final run

Double-Poling
Keys to Success Checklist

Ask a trained observer—an instructor, a coach, or a knowledgeable skier—to observe each phase of your double poling for efficiency. She or he should also observe the overall sequence to check for flowing motion that is free of glitches or strain. Use the checklist in Figure 3.1 to evaluate your performance and provide a prescription for improvement.

Step 4   No-Pole Skating

Once you feel comfortable with the speed at which you glide across the snow in the diagonal stride, it's time to try skating, an alternative way to generate momentum on flat terrain. No-pole skating is an excellent place to start exploring freestyle skiing. Because it requires no poling, you can concentrate upon just the skating action of the feet, which makes your learning easier.

In no-pole skating, the skis move away from parallel alignment into a V shape. This stance may be more intimidating at first, because it requires greater control of the skis, but new skiers ultimately find skating to be an exhilarating experience, especially if they like to ski fast!

Skating can generate more speed with less energy than the diagonal stride, because the V shape of the skis enables you to strongly push off the ski edge for momentum. This edge set provides a more solid platform for pushoff than the more subtle action of setting the wax against the snow in the diagonal stride. Setting the wax stops the ski momentarily, while a skater glides continuously even when pushing off.

Skating on a ski without kick wax or a patterned base is the best way to learn freestyle moves, because it eliminates any grab against the snow and enhances glide. But new skiers can learn skating basics on the same skis with which they are striding and double-poling, regardless of the base, if the snow is groomed into a hard, packed surface. It's best to avoid skating in new, soft snow, where the skis catch and slow down because of the abrasive conditions. Ski areas sometimes restrict skating to specific trails, and skaters should observe this courtesy to traditional skiers.

WHY IS NO-POLE SKATING IMPORTANT?

No-pole skating encourages the development of the most important skiing skill—the ability to balance and glide on one ski—and it can dramatically improve your performance of other maneuvers. The V shape forces you to balance on only one ski at a time as you shift your weight from ski to ski to move forward. You cannot compromise your weight transfer and shuffle along with both skis on the snow, which the diagonal stride allows.

Although new skiers can feel insecure when first learning to skate, the reward is ultimately very high. The improved ability to glide on each ski improves performance of the diagonal stride. Now you are able to firmly commit yourself to one ski at a time and glide longer on each ski, making your diagonal stride more efficient. Your ability to move your legs independently of each other is also valuable when you progress to moves on the hill. With its reliance upon a nonparallel stance, skating sets the stage well for downhill maneuvers. You will be more comfortable steering your skis into the converging shapes of wedges and christie turns if you've already experienced a departure from parallel alignment on flat terrain—without the added variable of downhill speed.

No-pole skating allows you to develop a foundation for more advanced freestyle skiing. The basic stance forms a common thread through every skating maneuver. Pay careful attention to basic skills here, for these will benefit you greatly when you are ready for the faster skating techniques. Establishing an efficient skating stance is an important introductory step.

HOW TO SKATE WITHOUT POLES

The key to no-pole skating is effective weight transfer, where you shift your body completely over each ski without rocketing quickly off the inside edges of the skis. Complete weight transfer requires a square stance over the ski; your head, hips, and feet are aligned over the ski, and your torso faces in the same direction as the ski tip (see Figure 4.1, a-d). Your shoulders and hips swivel as one unit to face in the new direction.

If you have aligned your body properly, it will be centered over a flat ski that allows you to pause and hold your balance over the ski. If you fall quickly off the inside edge of the ski, pausing momentarily or not at all, then your body is straddling the snow inside the V of the skis. Commit your weight completely to the ski by making sure every body part is stacked over the ski.

Use a narrow V shape with your first skating strides to shorten the distance your weight must be shifted. The narrower stance keeps your skis flatter on the snow and promotes subtler body actions with smoother, gentler glide. A wide V forces you to aggressively shift your weight side to side to be centered over the skis; the wider shape also edges the skis more strongly and generates more momentum. Use a more aggressive V shape only after you've experienced smooth weight transfer.

Another important consideration in no-pole skating is gliding, rather than stepping, onto each ski when the weight shift occurs. Smooth, efficient skating feels like you are waltzing from ski to ski and skimming the ski forward when you move onto it. Avoid a downward step that sends the force into the snow and diminishes forward speed.

Figure 4.1 Keys to Success: No-Pole Skating

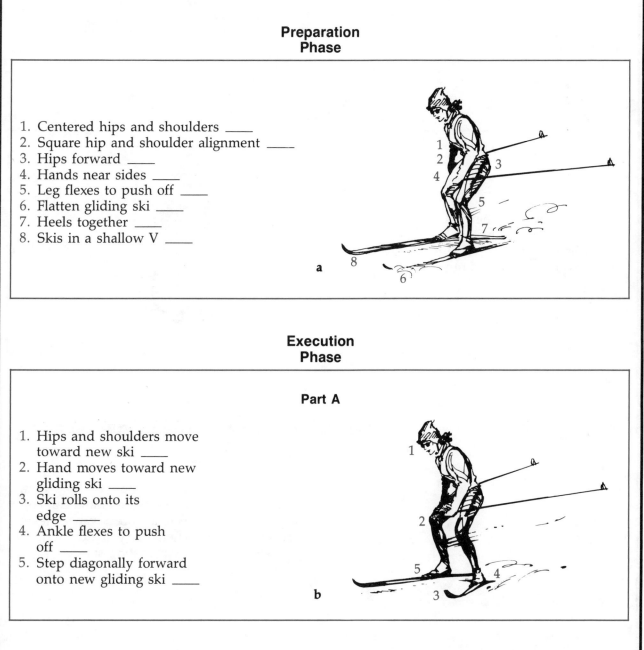

Preparation Phase

1. Centered hips and shoulders ____
2. Square hip and shoulder alignment ____
3. Hips forward ____
4. Hands near sides ____
5. Leg flexes to push off ____
6. Flatten gliding ski ____
7. Heels together ____
8. Skis in a shallow V ____

Execution Phase

Part A

1. Hips and shoulders move toward new ski ____
2. Hand moves toward new gliding ski ____
3. Ski rolls onto its edge ____
4. Ankle flexes to push off ____
5. Step diagonally forward onto new gliding ski ____

**Execution
Phase**

Part B

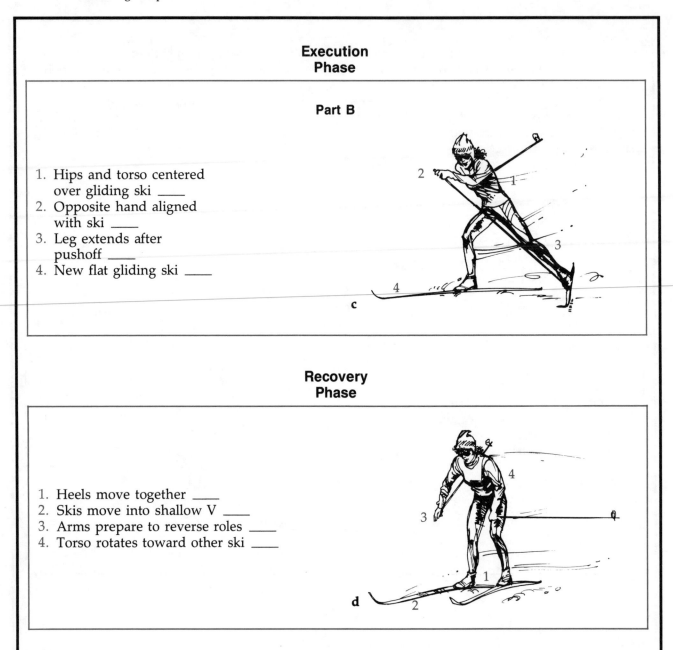

1. Hips and torso centered over gliding ski ____
2. Opposite hand aligned with ski ____
3. Leg extends after pushoff ____
4. New flat gliding ski ____

**Recovery
Phase**

1. Heels move together ____
2. Skis move into shallow V ____
3. Arms prepare to reverse roles ____
4. Torso rotates toward other ski ____

Detecting Errors in No-Pole Skating

These problems are common to all skating moves, not just no-pole skating, and can continue to cause errors at a more advanced level. Use this section whenever you experience a problem with the basic skating stance.

ERROR 🚫	CORRECTION
1. Straddling the snow within the V shape makes weight transfer inefficient.	1. Center your weight directly over your foot by aligning your toes, knee, and nose. Flatten the ski against the snow.
2. A lack of shoulder and hip swivel interferes with centering your body over the ski.	2. Swivel your shoulders and hips fully by aligning your jacket zipper over the new gliding ski.
3. Your legs fail to come together when riding the gliding ski, which shortens glide.	3. Tap your heels together. Bring your knees together, also, to ensure a straighter leg.
4. You step downward onto the ski rather than gliding forward onto it.	4. Keep the ski low to the snow, and "scuff" it forward before moving onto it. Keep your leg straight as you glide onto the ski. Bending your leg lifts the ski from the snow and encourages stepping.

No-Pole Skating Drills

1. Rocking Drill

With your skis in a V shape, rock gently from ski to ski, in place. Keep your legs comfortably straight, letting them bend naturally as you move between the skis. Pause momentarily over each ski to hold your balance, bringing your legs close together to keep your body centered over the ski. Keep the ski flat to balance over it. Strive for a smooth rhythm with weight transfer.

Success Goal = 10 repetitions without wobbling

Your Score = (#) ____ repetitions

2. Toe-Knee-Nose Drill

Continue to rock gently from ski to ski, in place. Hold your position over each ski by aligning your nose above your knee, which is above your toes (see Figures a and b). Think of your spine as a central axis to be shifted directly over the ski. Stay flat-footed on the ski, with a straight ankle.

Success Goal = 10 repetitions without wobbling

Your Score = (#) ____ repetitions

a

b

3. Zipper Swivel Drill

Continue to rock gently from ski to ski, in place. Keep your hips and shoulders square to the tip of each ski, and focus on feeling the swivel of these parts over the new ski. Use your jacket zipper as a point of orientation, and position your zipper directly over each ski as you stand on it.

   An alternative is using your chest as a set of headlights. Point those headlights in the same direction as your ski tip. Be careful to swing your hips as well as your shoulders.

Success Goal = 10 repetitions with complete swivel

Your Score = (#) _____ repetitions

4. Scuffing Drill

Begin to move forward by scuffing your skis gently against the snow as you step forward. Glide on each ski very briefly to maintain balance. Strive for a balanced scuff forward rather than long, powerful skating steps. Let your glide lengthen naturally as you develop comfort riding the glide ski.

Success Goal = 50 yards of scuff skating without falling

Your Score = (#) _____ yards of scuff skating

5. Narrow-to-Wide Angle Drill

Increase the width of the V created by your skis, and watch the edges dig into the snow more sharply. Now you have a good platform from which to push off more strongly. Ski down the trail, and prepare to push off harder by flexing at the ankle and knee. This action ''preloads'' your muscles like a coiled spring and provides greater power. Push only as hard as you can while still maintaining your balance on each gliding ski.

Success Goal = 50 yards of wide-angle skating with good balance

Your Score = (#) _____ yards of wide-angle skating

6. Foot-Tap Drill

When skating with a wider V shape, you have to recapture a closed stance with your legs after pushing off. Bring your trailing (straight) leg next to your gliding leg until you can tap your heels together. The tapping helps center your body over the ski to improve balance.

You may feel a difference in how close your feet come together on alternate strides, because it's common to have a stronger gliding leg. You'll be able to tap your heels when gliding on the stronger leg. But the weaker leg may shorten the glide on that ski and prevent you from tapping your feet together. Either bring the trailing leg over more quickly to get centered over the ski, or return to one-legged balance drills with the weaker leg.

Success Goal = 10 consecutive foot taps

Your Score = (#) _____ foot taps

7. Skating Lane Drill

Skate gently for 25 yards and examine your path. You should be able to see the width of your path (the point of farthest glide from side to side) by the tracks left in the snow (see Figure a). Ski along the same stretch, and widen your skating lane slightly by pushing off harder and gliding longer. You'll be able to see the new, longer skating tracks (see Figure b).

Repeat this drill until you cannot widen the skating lane any farther or the rhythm of your skating is undermined by trying to glide excessively.

a   b

Success Goal = Widening your skating lane as much as possible

Your Score = (#) _____ feet wider than first attempt

8. Ball-Passing Drill

Skate down a groomed 100-yard field with a partner, and pass a soccer ball between you. Use your foot or your ski to hit the ball to your partner. The passing requires quick reflexes in changing from skating to kicking.

The drill encourages flexibility in the legs, improves one-legged balance, and develops the ability to change direction quickly without your consciously thinking about it.

Success Goal = 200 yards of ball passing

Your Score = (#) _____ yards of ball passing

No-Pole Skating
Keys to Success Checklist

The major area to check is your basic stance. Ask a trained observer—an instructor, a coach, or a knowledgeable skier—to see if your body is centered correctly over the skis. This "toe-knee-nose" stance enables you to ride out forward momentum and remain balanced. The next area is creating more powerful skating by pushing off each ski more strongly and gliding longer on each ski. Use the checklist in Figure 4.1 to analyze your performance and provide appropriate solutions.

Step 5 **Climbing and Descending Gentle Hills**

Once you feel comfortable moving forward on flat terrain, it's time to explore new territory. Gentle trails with dips and rises in terrain are the next step in your development as a cross-country skier. Learning to climb uphill efficiently is an important consideration, because it reduces the fatigue and frustration that can result from excessive slipping on the hills.

Descending hills on cross-country skis is an exhilarating experience when you ski them safely. The best descents are those where you feel comfortable with the speed and confident in your ability to control the momentum. The same gentle terrain where you're ready to climb hills is the appropriate place to gain experience with safe descents.

Choose a hill with an adequate run-out that allows you to coast naturally to a complete stop. Avoid a run-out with a corner at the bottom or any obstacles that force you to stop quickly. You want the gentle pitch of the hill to slow your momentum. The gentler the hill, the more easily you will become comfortable with descending. Passively riding out the hill's momentum gives you the opportunity to develop effective balance while moving quickly. A steeper hill or a short run-out forces you to actively control momentum, which is a more complex task. Remember that one person's molehill can be another person's mountain! Begin with extremely gentle grades, and increase to more difficult slopes only when you can control the ascent and descent.

Climbing Gentle Hills

The two most common maneuvers for moving uphill are the sidestep and the herringbone. Each provides a slow but secure means of climbing hills. Sidestepping requires that you keep the skis parallel and across the fall line (the imaginary line that follows the greatest angle of the hill) as you move uphill (see Figure 5.1, a and b). You edge your skis against the snow to provide a stable platform from which to step sideways up the hill. The herringbone uses a distinctive V shape with the skis, and the pattern created in the snow resembles the skeleton of a fish (see Figure 5.2, a and b). Angle your skis in a V, and step forward up the hill, digging the skis' inside edges into the snow to get traction.

WHY ARE THE SIDESTEPPING AND HERRINGBONE MANEUVERS IMPORTANT?

Sidestepping is the slowest way to move uphill, but it lets you eat up a hill's elevation one bite at a time. Using the edges of the skis for traction is a more secure way to climb than the herringbone or the diagonal stride. Even if you begin to slip sideways, you can edge your skis or gently lean into the hill and fall down under control. It's important to learn sidestepping at the outset, because it's also a good option for descending a steep hill. You might need to sidestep down only the steepest part at the top before you feel comfortable riding out the remainder of the hill with another maneuver. Sidestepping lets you make the right choice to enhance your safety.

The herringbone provides you with an easier, quicker means of climbing uphill. You use the V of your skis to obtain a good edge from which to step forward up the hill. Each step of the herringbone moves you farther up the hill than sidestepping's short step. The herringbone is an important transition to more aggressive uphill climbing. The V provides more solid traction than the diagonal stride, where you run uphill and rely upon the subtler action of setting your wax pocket against the snow to move forward. The herringbone is an appropriate middle step in learning how to step up the hill fluidly with less risk of slipping backward.

HOW TO EXECUTE THE SIDESTEP

Begin at the bottom of the hill on flat terrain with your skis perpendicular to the fall line (across the hill). Flex at your ankles and knees, and swing your knees from side to side. Watch your skis roll from edge to edge. Moving your knees actually moves your entire lower leg, and you should feel your ankles also tipping into the hill to set the ski on edge. This edge control becomes important as the steepness of the hill increases. You increase the movement of your knees into the hill to prevent slipping (see Figure 5.1a).

Take small steps sideways, keeping your skis parallel to each other and perpendicular to the fall line. Keep your poles outside your skis, so you can plant them while you are stepping, to improve balance. Stay erect but relaxed over your skis, and look around to remain aware of the fall line (see Figure 5.1b). The most difficult part of sidestepping is understanding how fall lines can change. Imagine a ball rolling down the hill, taking the path of least resistance, and you will understand how the line can zigzag. You have to adjust the perpendicular orientation of your skis to the fall line as the line changes. This means moving the ski tips or tails farther up the hill to prevent slipping backward or forward down the hill.

Figure 5.1 Keys to Success: Sidestep

FOCUS KEY

Preparation Phase

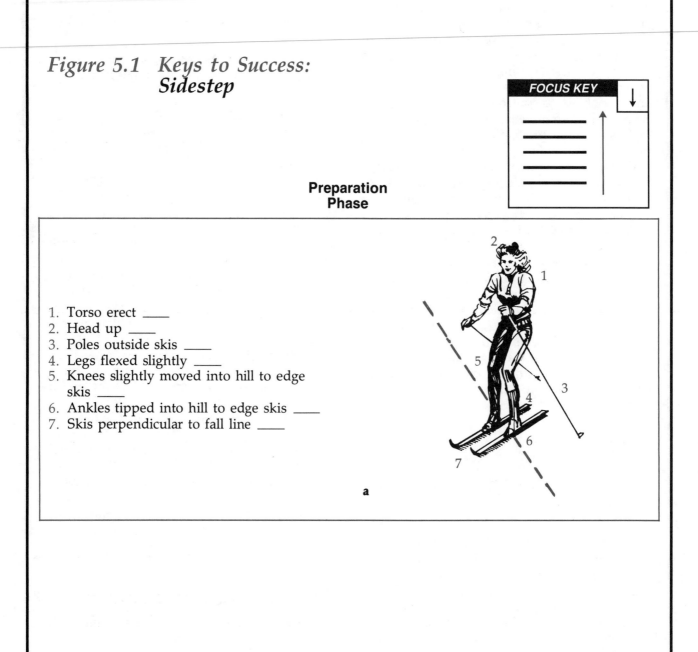

1. Torso erect ____
2. Head up ____
3. Poles outside skis ____
4. Legs flexed slightly ____
5. Knees slightly moved into hill to edge skis ____
6. Ankles tipped into hill to edge skis ____
7. Skis perpendicular to fall line ____

a

Execution
Phase

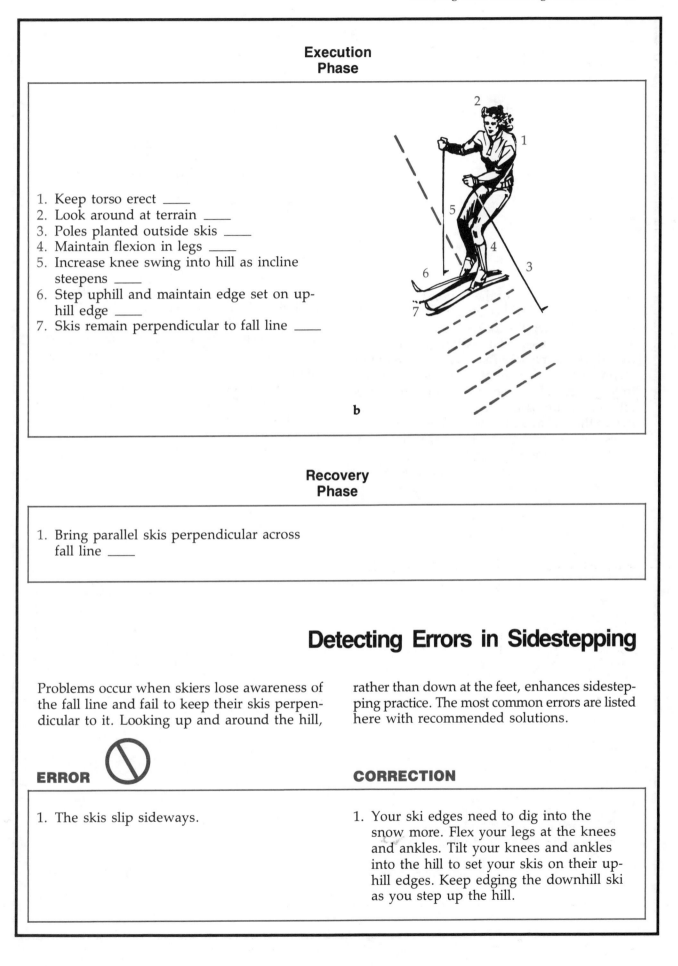

1. Keep torso erect ____
2. Look around at terrain ____
3. Poles planted outside skis ____
4. Maintain flexion in legs ____
5. Increase knee swing into hill as incline steepens ____
6. Step uphill and maintain edge set on up-hill edge ____
7. Skis remain perpendicular to fall line ____

b

Recovery
Phase

1. Bring parallel skis perpendicular across fall line ____

Detecting Errors in Sidestepping

Problems occur when skiers lose awareness of the fall line and fail to keep their skis perpendicular to it. Looking up and around the hill, rather than down at the feet, enhances sidestepping practice. The most common errors are listed here with recommended solutions.

ERROR

CORRECTION

1. The skis slip sideways.

1. Your ski edges need to dig into the snow more. Flex your legs at the knees and ankles. Tilt your knees and ankles into the hill to set your skis on their up-hill edges. Keep edging the downhill ski as you step up the hill.

ERROR   **CORRECTION**

2. The tips or tails slide downhill.

2. Your skis are no longer perpendicular to the fall line. Look around the hill. If you've slipped backward, move the tails farther up the hill. If you've slipped forward, move the tips farther up the hill.

HOW TO EXECUTE THE HERRINGBONE

Begin at the bottom of the hill on the flat run-out, and move your skis into a V. Rock from ski to ski, and watch the inside edges dig into the snow. Your ankles roll inward slightly to dig in the edges sharply. Begin to walk up the hill by stepping forward enough to prevent the tails from hitting and clicking. Swing your arms naturally in an alternate fashion, just like in walking up the hill, and push your poles against the snow outside the V of your skis and behind your body (see Figure 5.2, a and b).

Keep your body erect in the herringbone, and look at the top of the hill or at treetops. Keep-ing your head up tucks in your buttocks, which keeps your weight directly over the center of your skis. Bending at the waist shifts your weight backward, which encourages slipping and prevents you from stepping far enough up the hill to step free of the other ski. When the tails click, you are usually taking small steps sideways rather than moderate steps up the hill.

The shape of the V varies according to the steepness of the hill. A steeper hill requires a wider V, because greater edging of the skis is necessary to prevent slipping. A narrower V on gentler terrain blends fluidly into the diagonal stride on top of the hill.

Figure 5.2   *Keys to Success:* *Herringbone*

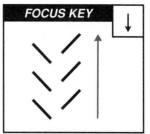

Preparation Phase

1. Torso erect _____
2. Look at top of hill _____
3. Skis in V _____
4. Ski on inside edge _____
5. Center your weight on ski _____
6. Poles angled behind body _____
7. Move uplifted ski up the hill _____

**Execution
Phase**

1. Keep torso erect ____
2. Look at top of hill ____
3. Step forward uphill ____
4. Center your weight on ski ____
5. Plant poles outside the skis ____

**Transition
Phase**

1. Step up the hill onto other ski ____

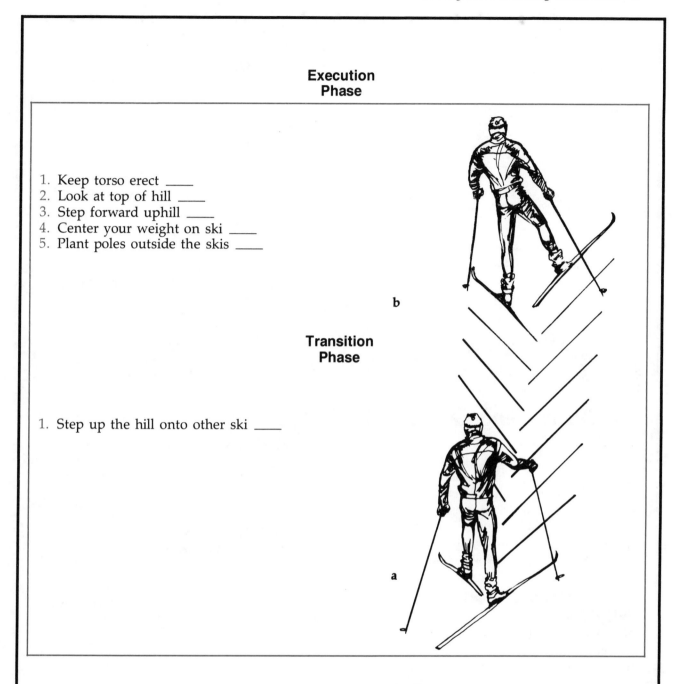

b

a

Detecting Errors in the Herringbone

Looking down at the snow, rather than at the top of the hill, is also a common problem with the herringbone. Keep aware of the entire hill environment, by standing upright and looking around, so you can handle the terrain more effectively.

ERROR ⊘	CORRECTION
1. The skis slip backward.	1. Inadequate edging promotes slipping. Stand upright to tuck your buttocks under your torso, and look at the top of the hill. Flex your legs and roll your ankles slightly inward to edge the skis.
2. The tails click.	2. Step forward up, up, up the hill rather than sideways. Standing erect brings your hips forward and enables you to step forward more easily.
3. The poles are planted weakly.	3. Keep the poles angled behind your body, outside the V of the skis. Avoid an upright pole plant, because you cannot push against it to move uphill.

Descending Gentle Hills

A straight run is the first maneuver to practice when descending the hill. This basic move lets you develop the key skills that are the foundation of all downhill moves. The more time you spend with straight descents, the better your success with the more advanced hill techniques.

WHY IS THE STRAIGHT RUN IMPORTANT?

A straight run isolates the basic balanced stance that you will use in all downhill moves, and it simplifies an introduction to the hill. In a straight run, the skis remain parallel to provide maximum lateral stability and improve comfort. More advanced downhill moves require that you move the skis into angled positions involving more complex leg movements. These moves, like learning to stop or turn, come later in the process.

Repeated practice of straight runs reinforces the efficient elements of the basic skiing stance, which provides a solid foundation for advanced moves. Develop good habits here, and you will reap big rewards later.

An emphasis on straight runs in the beginning allows you to relax, which is a very important element in skiing. You might be tense if you are afraid of falling. With repeated exposure to a gentle hill, you will be more comfortable with gliding speed and falling. It's inevitable that new skiers will fall on hills, but the best introduction is a low-speed, controlled fall rather than a high-speed, uncontrolled crash.

HOW TO DESCEND IN A STRAIGHT RUN

To balance on their gliding skis, skiers use an all-purpose stance familiar to many athletes. They relax their bodies into a slightly lowered position that readies them for a move in any direction.

The quiet torso is erect but relaxed; avoid a tiring arch in your back or a bend at the waist. Tilt the pelvic area, which scoops the hips forward, tucks in the buttocks, and settles the spine into a comfortable position.

Flex your legs comfortably with a slight bend at your knees and ankles to act like shock absorbers with changes in terrain. Keep your hands low and in front of your thighs to preserve a low center of gravity. Look up and down the hill rather than at your skis.

The best stance on narrow cross-country skis is a wide one for maximum lateral stability; spread your feet until they are slightly less than shoulder-width apart. Stand flat-footed on the skis, and settle your weight between your heels and toes (see Figure 5.3).

Figure 5.3 Keys to Success:
Straight Run

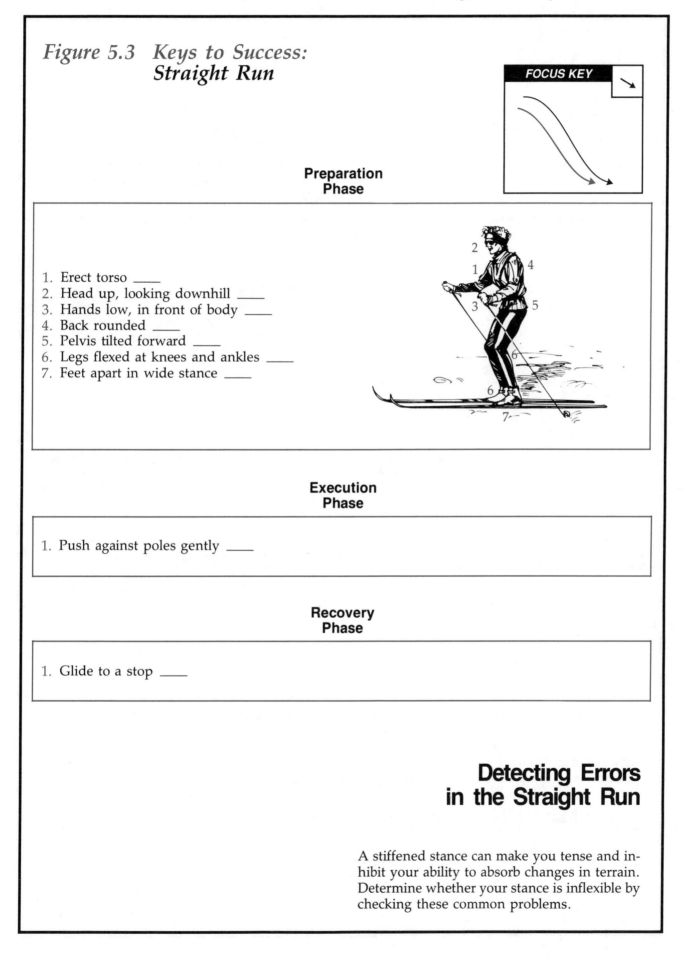

FOCUS KEY

**Preparation
Phase**

1. Erect torso ____
2. Head up, looking downhill ____
3. Hands low, in front of body ____
4. Back rounded ____
5. Pelvis tilted forward ____
6. Legs flexed at knees and ankles ____
7. Feet apart in wide stance ____

**Execution
Phase**

1. Push against poles gently ____

**Recovery
Phase**

1. Glide to a stop ____

Detecting Errors
in the Straight Run

A stiffened stance can make you tense and inhibit your ability to absorb changes in terrain. Determine whether your stance is inflexible by checking these common problems.

ERROR 🚫   **CORRECTION**

ERROR	CORRECTION
1. Stiff ankles and knees prevent your legs from absorbing bumps in the terrain.	1. Bend your knees and especially your ankles to lower your stance. Keep the joints flexible to absorb shock.
2. Bending at your waist undermines front-to-back stability.	2. Stand erect, and drop your spine straight downward by bending only your legs.
3. Your hands wave erratically.	3. Some hand movement is fine at first to help you stay balanced. But strive to bring your hands in front of your body and low near your thighs.
4. Too much weight rests on your heels, causing a backward fall.	4. Stiff ankles keep your body upright and back toward your heels. Bend at the ankles to shift your weight toward your toes without lifting your heels from the skis.

Climbing and Descending Gentle Hills Drills

Do the following drills in pairs (ascent and descent) so that you have a focus for both ascending and descending the same gentle practice hill. Choose a gentle incline with a flat run-out area that allows you to coast to a stop.

1. Railroad Tracks Drill (Ascend)

On the flat run-out at the base of a hill, establish two tracks that are an extension of the fall line. Use the tracks as a point of orientation, and stand on them with your skis perpendicular to the line. Take sideways steps and maintain the perpendicular alignment. Look ahead at the snow rather than at your feet. Examine your ski tracks to determine whether you maintained the perpendicular orientation. Continue sidestepping up the hill.

Success Goal = 10 sidesteps with perpendicular orientation

Your Score = (#) _____ sidesteps with perpendicular orientation

2. Slump and Slouch (Descend)

Stand flat-footed on the skis with your feet side by side. Stiffen your body, and then release this tension by bending your legs and slumping into a lower, stable stance. Round your shoulders, and tilt your pelvis forward by tightening your buttocks. Descend a gentle hill in this position.

Success Goal = 1 straight run in slumped position

Your Score = (#) _____ straight run

3. Blind Sidestepping (Ascend)

On the flat run-out at the base of a hill, close your eyes to sidestep. Try to feel the parallel alignment of your skis by concentrating upon the parallel positioning of your feet. Sidestep uphill with your eyes closed. If you slip, analyze the ski tracks left in the snow and change your foot orientation to improve the ski alignment.

Success Goal = 10 sidesteps with parallel alignment

Your Score = (#) _____ sidesteps with parallel alignment

4. High-Low Drill (Descend)

Stand flat-footed on your skis with a slight bend in your ankles, which creates a high stance. Begin to descend a gentle hill, and bend your ankles and knees increasingly as your speed increases. This strategy lowers your center of gravity and improves balance. Strive for a smooth transition as you change from high to low stances. End the run as low as possible without bending excessively forward at the waist. Let your bent legs create the low position.

Success Goal = 1 straight run, changing from a high to a low stance

Your Score = (#) _____ straight run

5. Bend-and-Step Drill (Ascend)

Begin to climb a gentle hill with sidestepping, and exaggerate leg bend at your ankles and knees. Point your bent knees into the hill to emphasize edging. If you slip at any point, remember to exaggerate the up-and-down bending as well as the knee swing into the hill. Exaggerated knee swing makes sure your ankles are also rolling into the hill to improve the edge set.

Success Goal = 1 ascent with exaggerated bending

Your Score = (#) _____ ascent with exaggerated bending

6. Ankle Angles Drill (Descend)

Stand tall on your skis with your shins creating a 90-degree angle with the skis (see Figure a). Create a smaller angle between your shins and skis by bending your ankles (see Figures b and c). Flex your ankles smoothly to create smaller angles (to lower your body) and larger angles (to raise your body). Strive for smooth changes in ankle flexion, and always flex them greatly when you become unbalanced.

Descend a gentle hill, and call out different angles to yourself (90 degrees, 65 degrees, 45 degrees, etc.). Raise and lower your stance smoothly without lifting your heels from the skis.

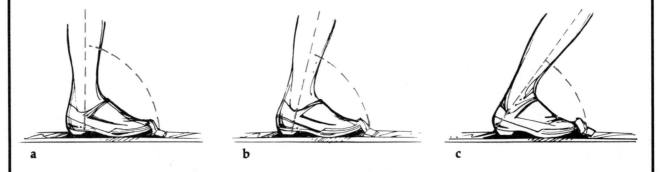

a   b   c

Success Goal = 1 straight run with 5 changes in ankle flexion

Your Score = (#) _____ changes in ankle flexion

7. Half-Herringbone Traverse (Ascend)

Prepare to ascend a broad hill on a diagonal path from one corner at the bottom to the opposite corner at the top of a hill. The hill rises more gently along this path than in a straight uphill attack and lets you control your skis more easily.

The traverse provides a good transition from the sidestep to a full herringbone.

Use a half-V formation with your skis when you begin to climb. The uphill ski remains aligned with the diagonal path. The downhill ski stays perpendicular to the fall line, acting as a brake and creating a platform from which you can securely step forward along the diagonal route.

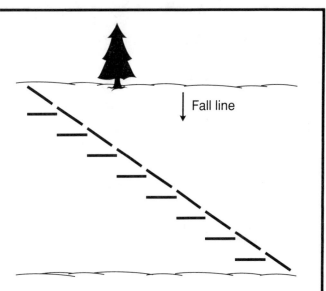

Fall line

Success Goal = 1 ascent with no slippage

Your Score = (#) _____ half herringbones
  with no slippage

8. Bobbing Partners (Descend)

Hold hands with a partner, and descend a gentle hill together. Raise and lower your stances in unison, bending and extending the ankles smoothly. Quick pops upward can send your weight up and backward, which can result in a fall. Bob slowly for better balance.

Holding onto a partner increases lateral stability, but be ready to move apart if one person becomes unbalanced and falls.

Success Goal = 2 straight runs with a partner, bobbing in unison

  a. 1 straight run, counting initial number of bobs

  b. 1 straight run, increasing number of bobs

Your Score =

  a. (#) _____ total bobs in first run

  b. (#) _____ total bobs in second run

9. Zigzag Traverse (Ascend)

Traverse the hill in a zigzag manner, which involves changes in direction. When following a diagonal line up the hill, use the half herringbone. To change direction, take small steps to round the corner. Midway through the corner, you'll be in a full herringbone position where your inside edges will dig most sharply into the snow to prevent sliding.

Traverse the hill the first time with a gentler, more gradual path that requires fewer turns. Then traverse more directly up the hill during a second ascent, with shorter, quicker traverses.

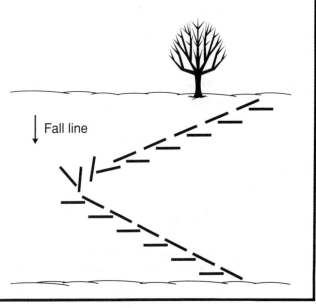

Fall line

Success Goal = 2 ascents with a zigzag traverse

   a. 1 traverse with several changes in direction

   b. 1 traverse with a greater number of changes in direction

Your Score =

   a. (#) ____ changes in direction on first traverse

   b. (#) ____ changes in direction on second traverse

10. Hand Control Drill (Descend)

Descend a gentle hill with your hands on your waist. When you feel comfortably balanced on your skis, slide your hands forward and low as if you were holding a steering wheel.

Success Goal = 1 straight run with quiet hands

Your Score = (#) ____ straight run with quiet hands

11. Duck Walk (Ascend)

At the base of a hill, move your skis into a V shape like a duck's webbed feet and prepare to approach the hill. If you walk naturally in the V formation with an alternate swing of the arms, the action resembles a duck's waddling. Rotate your hips around with each step to aid your weight shift between the skis.

   Keep your skis in a narrow V on flat terrain to move forward easily, and then widen the V gradually for better traction as you ascend the hill. As the hill steepens, exaggerate your waddling to promote more effective weight transfer from ski to ski. This encourages a firm step up the hill that prevents slipping.

Success Goal = 1 ascent in which you exaggerate the waddling at the hill's midpoint to experience better weight transfer

Your Score = (#) ____ herringbones with exaggerated weight transfer

12. One-Legged Drill (Descend)

Descend a gentle hill, and rock from ski to ski by shifting most of your weight over each ski. This forces you to balance primarily on the ski supporting most of your weight. Keep your leg flexed at the ankle and knee to maintain good balance. Press gently on the unweighted ski to keep a little weight on it and control it. Feel your weight shift from side to side, directly over the supporting skis.

Success Goal = 2 straight runs, rocking from ski to ski

    a. 1 straight run, counting initial number of weight transfers

    b. 1 straight run, increasing number of weight transfers

Your Score =

    a. (#) _____ weight shifts in first run

    b. (#) _____ weight shifts in second run

13. Beat Your Tracks (Ascend)

Choose a packed hill section covered with light snow, and herringbone in a relaxed manner up the hill. Analyze your tracks to discover how far you stepped forward up the hill, which should be evident in the snow. Ascend the hill again, and step above your original tracks to lengthen your step.

    If the snow is too hard to leave obvious tracks, ask another person to estimate the size of your step. Try to increase the step by several inches, with the other person observing your herringbone to determine how much farther you have increased the step.

Success Goal = An increase in the length of your herringbone step up the hill

Your Score =

    a. (#) _____ inches of original step

    b. (#) _____ inches of subsequent step

14. Two-Step Drill (Descend)

Descend a gentle hill, and take a tiny step sideways to follow a new route downhill. To enhance balance, keep your legs bent as you step and settle into the new straight running position. Take more than one step sideways if you feel comfortable doing so.

Success Goal = 1 straight run with a sideways step

Your Score = (#) _____ sideways steps

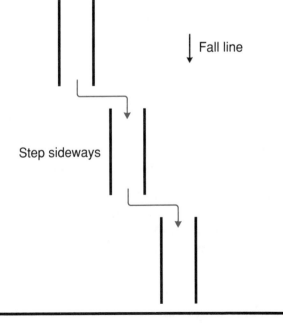
Fall line
Step sideways

15. Run Herringbone (Ascend)

This aggressive version of the herringbone takes more energy, but it gets you up the hill more quickly. Charge the hill with a quicker tempo, and bound from ski to ski.

First ascend the hill in a casual manner, and count the number of herringbone steps. Then ascend the hill quickly with the run herringbone, and count the number of steps. The number will be lower, because the bounding encourages you to spring forward and farther up the hill.

Success Goal = A decrease in the number of herringbone steps to reach the hilltop

Your Score =

  a. (#) _____ casual herringbone steps to reach the hilltop

  b. (#) _____ run herringbone steps to reach the hilltop

16. Diagonal Traverse (Descend)

Prepare to descend a steeper hill by skiing from one top corner to the opposite corner at the bottom. The diagonal line, which cuts across the fall line, reduces the speed of the descent. As you descend, move your knees slightly into the hill to dig the ski edges into the snow and prevent skidding. Keep your legs flexed at the ankle and knee. Face your shoulders slightly down the hill to counter the leg movement into the hill—your stance will feel more secure.

Success Goal = 1 diagonal traverse

Your Score = (#) _____ diagonal traverse

17. Gliding Herringbone (Ascend)

This variation gets you up the hill more easily, because you add a little glide to each step. It requires a more aggressive transfer of weight from ski to ski to push the ski uphill and increase glide by a few inches.

Exaggerated hip motion improves the glide. Each time you step onto the ski, swing your hips strongly onto the ski and use the momentum to push the ski tip farther up the hill.

Look at the width of your original herringbone path. Ascend the hill with a gliding herringbone, and watch how your glide widens your path slightly.

Success Goal = A wider herringbone path up the hill

Your Score =

  a. (#) ＿＿ feet of width in original herringbone path

  b. (#) ＿＿ inches increase in gliding herringbone ascent

18. Tuck the Hill (Descend)

Choose a straighter descent on this steeper hill, and use a tuck position to negotiate it. The tuck forces you to lean over with your elbows near your knees and your poles carried securely between your arms and body.

Although the tuck can increase your speed because it reduces wind resistance, it places you in a low, stable position that enhances balance. It also keeps you so low to the snow that you fall only a short distance if you lose your balance!

Success Goal = 1 straight run in a tuck

Your Score = (#) ＿＿ straight run in a tuck

Climbing and Descending Gentle Hills Keys to Success Checklists

Downhill slipping and excessive fatigue give you immediate feedback about your efficiency in climbing hills. Efficient hill climbing should feel stable and rhythmic with little slippage or stalling during the climb. Ask a trained observer—an instructor, a coach, or a knowledgeable skier—to analyze your sidestepping and herringbone maneuvers. Refer to the checklists in Figures 5.1 and 5.2 to determine the sources of any problems and appropriate corrections.

A relaxed, flexible stance is very important during straight run practice. Ask your observer to analyze your leg flexibility and posture so you can establish an effective stance before further downhill maneuvers. Your observer can use the checklist in Figure 5.3 to evaluate your straight run performance and provide feedback.

Step 6 Controlling Speed With the Wedge

Once you are comfortable with gentle descents, you need to learn how to control your speed in preparation for steeper hills. Variations on a basic wedge, sometimes called a snowplow, provide you with the means to control your descent on different types of hills. Once you finish practice of straight runs and feel comfortable with the incline of the hill, then you are ready to transfer these skills to the wedge.

Because some new skiers are apprehensive about hills, the best place to learn the wedge position is at the base of a hill on flat terrain. This strategy eliminates the added variable of speed and reduces apprehension so you can focus on key elements of the basic wedge position. Solidifying the stance here encourages a more successful transition to the hill.

Comfort during practice is reflected in relaxed, flexed legs, a quiet upper body, and hands low and in front of the body. This balanced position improves your ability to move your legs into the wedge, or snowplow, position and maintain it during the descent.

WHY IS THE WEDGE IMPORTANT?

The wedge is a new skier's primary means of increasing control on hills. Where increased steepness or a limited run-out prevents you from simply gliding downhill, the wedge lets you negotiate the hill safely. The angled position of your skis functions like a brake to slow your descent, and it reduces your likelihood of falling as a reaction to rapidly accelerating speed.

Learning the basic elements of the wedge also sets the stage for all advanced downhill moves. The mechanics of every turn can be related to the wedge and learned from this initial position. Developing solid skills in this move provides an important base for later success with other turns.

HOW TO EXECUTE A WEDGE

The basic wedge position is pie-shaped, with the ski tips pointing together and the tails pressed apart. Sink downward by flexing your legs at your ankles and knees, and slide your skis apart.

Rotate or twist your feet around to steer your skis into the wedge.

By relaxing and slumping your body, you support your weight with your skeleton rather than your muscles, which tense and tire. The same principles that you applied in the straight run are important here. Keep your torso erect with a rounded spine, and tilt your pelvis forward. Center your hips to keep your weight distributed equally between both skis. Keep your hands low and in front of your body with the poles angled backward out of the way (see Figure 6.1a).

Two types of wedges are important to new skiers: the gliding wedge and the braking wedge. The gliding wedge lets you ride out the hill's momentum (see Figure 6.1b), and the braking wedge controls speed more sharply (see Figure 6.1c).

The gliding wedge uses a comfortably high stance, where you flex your legs slightly to sink into the wedge. The shape of the wedge remains narrow, creating little edging of the skis against the snow. This reduced edging allows greater gliding and faster speeds. Begin your descent in a straight run, and then steer your skis into a narrow wedge.

The braking wedge uses a lower stance, where you bend your legs more deeply to lower yourself into the wedge. The shape of the wedge is wider, creating more edging against the snow. This increased resistance reduces gliding and inhibits speed. It usually evolves naturally out of a gliding wedge when you need to reduce your momentum.

The easiest way to learn the wedge is to start with the gliding wedge on a hill with a long, gentle run-out that allows you to coast to a stop. Because the gliding wedge uses more skeletal support and less muscular strength, it is an easier move for new skiers. The braking wedge involves more muscular control, so don't practice it until you are comfortable with the gliding wedge or the terrain demands it.

Because mastery of this move can be affected by tension, it is important to remain relaxed. Moving to a gentler hill may be necessary if the wedge feels uncomfortable. Tension tends to settle in the legs, which stiffen and lose their shock absorbency. Keep the legs flexed at the knees and at the ankles.

Wedges don't require the use of poles, but you may practice with them to make climbing hills easier. Simply hold them quietly and tucked out of the way during descents so they do not hinder performance. If you grip them tightly or wave them erratically, leave the poles to the side of the hill.

Figure 6.1 Keys to Success: Wedge

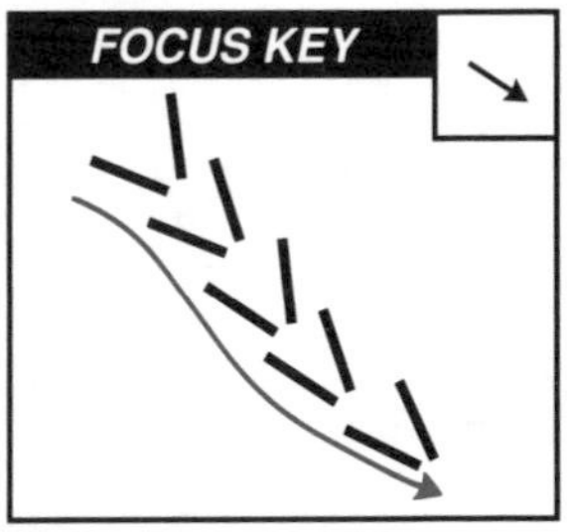

FOCUS KEY

Preparation Phase

Straight Run

1. Erect torso ____
2. Head up, looking downhill ____
3. Hands low, in front of body ____
4. Back rounded ____
5. Pelvis tilted forward ____
6. Legs flexed at knees and ankles ____
7. Feet apart in wide stance ____

a

Execution Phase

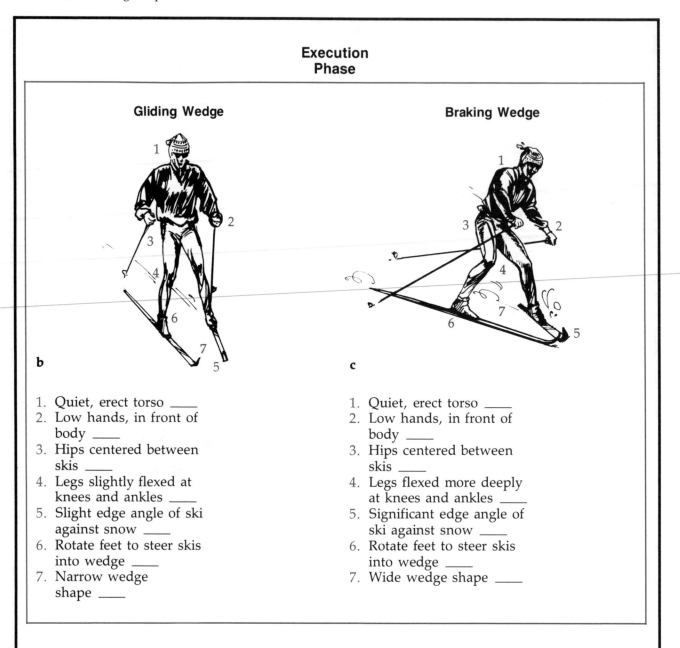

Gliding Wedge

b

1. Quiet, erect torso ____
2. Low hands, in front of body ____
3. Hips centered between skis ____
4. Legs slightly flexed at knees and ankles ____
5. Slight edge angle of ski against snow ____
6. Rotate feet to steer skis into wedge ____
7. Narrow wedge shape ____

Braking Wedge

c

1. Quiet, erect torso ____
2. Low hands, in front of body ____
3. Hips centered between skis ____
4. Legs flexed more deeply at knees and ankles ____
5. Significant edge angle of ski against snow ____
6. Rotate feet to steer skis into wedge ____
7. Wide wedge shape ____

Detecting Wedge Errors

The most common errors in wedges are outlined here with suggested methods to correct them. Body tension can affect your ability to properly execute a wedge. It is often created by being uneasy with the steepness of the practice hill. Be willing to move to a gentler hill if you have continuing problems with the wedge position. A return to exercises on flat terrain is also a valuable strategy.

ERROR	CORRECTION
1. You bend at the waist, sending your head forward and buttocks backward to obtain balance. Rocking can result.	1. Use erect posture to keep your torso upright and above your feet. This keeps your weight centered on the ski and in a neutral stance.
2. The shape of the wedge is lopsided, with one ski angled more than the other ski.	2. Steer each foot equally into the wedge with your weight centered between the skis. Rotate your feet simultaneously.
3. The tips of the skis chatter, and you experience an increase in momentum. You sit back on your skis.	3. Bend your ankles, but don't lift your heels from the skis. This weight shift forward puts more pressure on the front half of the skis for greater control.
4. One ski ''rails'' or over-edges and does not skid on the snow.	4. Repeat the skidding drills in Step 1. Now steer the flattened skis equally into the wedge and let them skid on the snow.
5. The ski edges do not dig into the snow to stop your accelerating speed.	5. Relax your stiffened, extended legs and bend them at the knees and ankles. This lowers your body, widens the wedge, and encourages greater edging.

Wedge Drills

1. Spread the Wedge

Use this in-place exercise on flat terrain to practice the basic wedge position. Step your skis into a pie shape with the tips close together and the tails farther apart. Bend at your knees and ankles and bob gently to relax your legs.

Return to a standing stance with your skis parallel. Your feet should be apart with a space between the skis. Push flat-footed against the skis to spread them apart and rotate your feet into a toe-in position. Both feet should steer equally to produce a symmetrical wedge shape.

Success Goal = Equal steering of each ski into the wedge position

Your Score = ____ Your judgment: How equal is your steering?

Blind-Eyed Wedge

Close your eyes and spread your skis into the wedge again. Focus on your feet pressing flat against the skis to move them apart, and turn your toes inward to shape the wedge. Settle your weight equally between the skis, and feel the bend at your ankles and knees. Open your eyes to check whether the wedge is symmetrical.

Success Goal = A symmetrical wedge shape

Your Score = _____ Your judgment: Have you formed a symmetrical wedge shape?

3. Partner Pushing

Ask a partner to remove his or her skis and prepare to push you across a flat, packed surface. The partner will push against your hips rather than your torso to avoid causing you to bend at the waist. Stay in a parallel stance at the outset to gain some speed, and then steer your skis into a narrow wedge.

Let the partner push you far enough so that you can raise and lower your stance, moving from a gliding wedge to a braking wedge. Concentrate on equal foot steering with your weight centered between the skis, and strive for smooth transitions between the two types of wedges. Finish off the practice by sinking low enough in a wide wedge to slow to a stop. Once you can brake to a complete stop, you are ready for the hill.

Success Goal = Smooth transitions from gliding to braking wedges

Your Score = _____ Your judgment: How smooth are your transitions?

4. Coast to a Stop

On a gentle hill, begin your descent with a straight run to glide smoothly. Then gently brush out your skis into a gliding wedge and ride out the momentum of the hill. Coast to a stop without applying any pressure or edging to brake with the skis. You may need to repeat this exercise several times before you can maintain a symmetrical wedge.

Success Goal = A gliding wedge with a symmetrical shape

Your Score = _____ Your judgment: How symmetrical is your gliding wedge?

5. Gliding Wedge Change-Ups

Once you feel comfortable gliding to a stop, experiment with wedge change-ups on the hill. From a straight run, sink gently into a gliding wedge for several feet, and then raise your body smoothly to let your skis run together again in a parallel stance. Repeat the sequence as many times as the hill allows, striving for smooth transitions between the wedge and the straight run to maintain good balance. Abrupt transitions can stiffen your legs and cause you to fall. Keep your ankles and knees flexible.

Success Goal = Smooth transitions between straight runs and gliding wedges

Your Score = _____ Your judgment: How smooth are your transitions?

Parallel stance

Gliding wedge

6. Tall-to-Small Wedges

Begin "tall" in a straight run, then sink gently into a gliding wedge to ride out the main pitch of the hill (see Figure a). As the run-out approaches, drop lower to a "small" stance to widen your wedge into a braking position (see Figure b). Press your feet against the edges of your skis to dig them in. Brake rather than coast to a stop on flat terrain at the base. Mark your ending point. (You can also think of this exercise in terms of the wedge shape: narrow, wide, wider.)

Repeat this exercise, and try to stop before your first end mark. Initiate your braking wedge earlier on the hill to do so. Then begin your braking wedge from the top of the hill to see how quickly you can brake to a stop.

Success Goal = Braking to a stop at three different points

Your Score =

a. (#) _____ yards to first end mark

b. (#) _____ yards to second end mark

c. (#) _____ yards to third end mark

7. *Countdown*

Use a number system for wedges of different widths. For instance, a 1 is the narrowest wedge and a 5 is the widest wedge. Descend the hill, and switch between different numbered wedges in a random order. Vary your stance from high to low by raising and lowering your body as you challenge yourself. Keep your legs limber as you change wedge positions. Another skier can also call out numbers as you descend the hill to provide a greater challenge.

Success Goal = Smooth transitions between gliding and braking wedges

Your Score = ____ Your judgment: How smooth are your transitions?

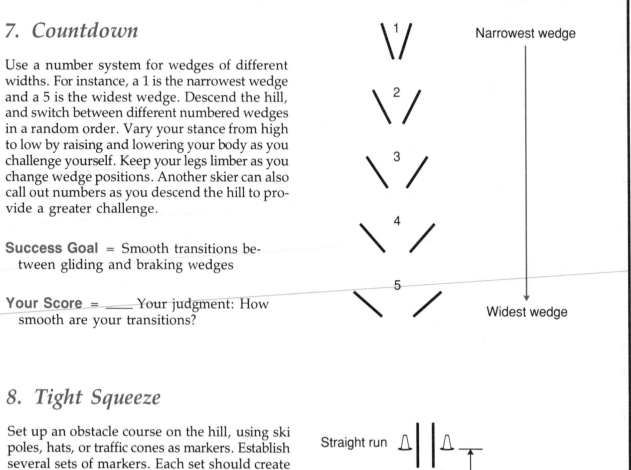

8. *Tight Squeeze*

Set up an obstacle course on the hill, using ski poles, hats, or traffic cones as markers. Establish several sets of markers. Each set should create a 1-yard opening, and the sets should be spaced about 10 feet apart on the hill. (The spacing can vary depending upon the speed of the snow: closer together on slower snow, farther apart on faster snow.)

Use a gliding wedge to descend the hill, and slide your skis into a parallel stance to squeeze between the first set of markers. After you pass through the markers, sink immediately into a wedge again before realigning your skis in a parallel position to negotiate the next set of markers.

The obstacle course forces you to react at specific spots, which readies you for more advanced terrain.

Success Goal = No touches on the obstacle course

Your Score = (#) ____ touches on the obstacle course

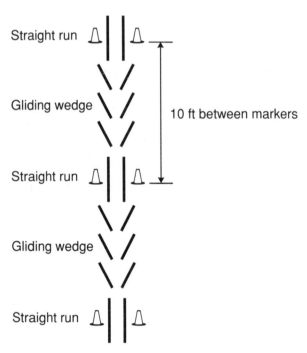

9. Red Light

Plant a pole at the base of the hill where the flat run-out begins, and attempt to stop just before this "red light." Use a gliding wedge to increase speed and to test the effectiveness of your braking wedge. Each time you stop successfully, move the pole farther up the hill—this forces you to stop on steeper terrain.

Success Goal = Improving your ability to stop quickly

Your Score = (#) _____ times you improved your ability to stop

Controlling Speed With the Wedge
Keys to Success Checklist

You will help control your speed on downhills by keeping your body relaxed and flexible so that you can maintain the wedge position despite bumps and dips in terrain. Control problems with wedges are directly related to body stiffness, which affects the basic stance and inhibits balance. Ask a trained observer—your instructor, a coach, or a knowledgeable skier—to determine whether your stance is flexible and symmetrical. Use the checklist in Figure 6.1 to evaluate your performance.

Step 7 Changing Direction With Turns

Once you've mastered speed control on straight descents, you can begin to prepare for steeper, curving trails that require more maneuvering. Your hill practice so far has helped make you comfortable keeping your balance while you're gliding and sets the stage for learning how to turn your skis to change direction and to avoid obstacles.

Changing direction is a more complex task than skiing straight downhill, because it requires a new combination of additional skills. To turn your skis, you must not only steer them into position while sliding but also transfer weight and edge the skis to complete the turns effectively.

Three types of turns are effective at this point in your development: wedge turns, step turns, and skate turns. Wedge turns are the best place to begin because they allow you to control your speed. Step turns and skate turns are faster moves that do not dampen speed, and you should be more comfortable on the hill before you try them.

WHY IS THE WEDGE TURN IMPORTANT?

The wedge turn relies on the already familiar wedge position, in which you can change the width of the position to control your speed as you change direction. A narrower shape, where you stand higher and use minimal edging, develops a faster series of turns that are easier to link. But you can lower your body into a wider wedge to increase edging and slow the speed of the turns. Good control is possible with a well-executed wedge turn.

The wedge turn is appropriate for packed snow and faster conditions, where the trail surface is relatively hard and the snow provides little resistance against the skis. Deeper snow makes it difficult, and often impossible, to steer your skis into the wedge position.

WHY IS THE STEP TURN IMPORTANT?

The step turn is often the best turn in softer, deeper snow conditions where steering the skis

into a wedge is difficult. The step turn, sometimes called "the turn of a thousand steps," is like taking many tiny steps around a corner. With each step, you lift the ski free of the snow and place it in the direction you want to go.

Whereas the wedge uses a converging position of the skis, the step turn uses a diverging step. It offers little speed control and requires that you ride out the momentum of a hill as you step around a corner. Effective in slower snow conditions, it becomes an exciting move when the snow is packed and fast.

A step turn emphasizes effective weight transfer from ski to ski, because you cannot straddle the skis during this move—you'd end up performing a split as the skis continued to move away from each other. The step turn relies upon a quick, crisp weight shift and good balance on one ski while gliding. This independent leg action sets the stage for learning more advanced turns later on.

WHY IS THE SKATE TURN IMPORTANT?

The skate turn is a natural extension of the step turn that you can begin practicing when you feel comfortable with the accelerated speed. Whereas the step turn passively uses the hill's momentum, the skate turn is a more active, aggressive move used in similar snow conditions. You can increase the speed at which you negotiate the corner, because the dynamics of the skate turn can actually generate momentum.

A skate turn relies upon good weight transfer, like the step turn, but it more strongly emphasizes the skills of edging and pushing off. You edge your skis sharply in the skate turn, creating a firmer platform from which to push off to move to the other ski. The turn reinforces independent leg action and introduces more aggressive pushing off. Skiers flex their legs to spring more dynamically from ski to ski.

HOW TO EXECUTE A WEDGE TURN

A good wedge position is crucial to the wedge turn. The best stance is a higher, gliding wedge with minimal edging, which reduces resistance against the snow and lets you steer the skis more easily (see Figure 7.1, a and b). If you try to turn from a braking wedge, the significant angle between the ski edges and the snow makes steering more difficult. If the steepness of the hill forces you to use a braking wedge, try to find a gentler hill for your initial turning practice. If you don't have the option of another hill, and braking wedges are necessary to control your speed, then you may have to practice more braking wedges before you attempt turns. You may also have to straighten your legs to initiate the turn. Your body will rise and flatten the skis against the snow, which reduces resistance against them. Then you can move easily and steer them in the new direction.

The first wedge turn can be as simple as looking in the desired direction of travel as you descend the hill and letting your legs follow your eyes. Begin in a gliding wedge with your skis relatively flat on the snow, and turn both legs in the direction you want to go. Moving the entire leg, particularly steering the feet, is important. Think of both knees and big toes pointing in the direction of the turn. It is especially important to steer the inside foot in the direction of the turn (see Figure 7.1, c-e). Keep your hips centered without any overt effort to shift weight or edge the skis. Keep the turn very close to the fall line,

with only a shallow change of direction through the fall line (see the Focus Key).

The next step is linking two turns, which requires a change in direction. Stay in the medium- or narrow-width wedge, where your flattened skis make it easier to change directions. Turn your legs in one direction until they have passed through the fall line, and return to a neutral wedge to complete the turn. Then direct your legs in the opposite direction. Keep your hips centered, your body high, and your torso quiet, to let the legs perform the steering. Keep the turns shallow so you won't need to steer much.

Once you've experienced this change in direction, you can experiment with more linked turns through the fall line. Increase the number of turns on the hill in small increments: Try three turns, and if successful, then four turns. Completing more turns requires that you steer the skis more quickly and change directions faster.

As you practice these linked turns, you may feel that your skis are edging naturally at the end of the turn. You may also experience a buildup of gravitational forces at this point and feel more pressure against the outside ski. These sensations are a natural result of effective turning. Don't focus on these elements, or they will undermine your ability to steer your skis from a balanced stance.

Figure 7.1   Keys to Success: *Wedge Turns*

Preparation Phase

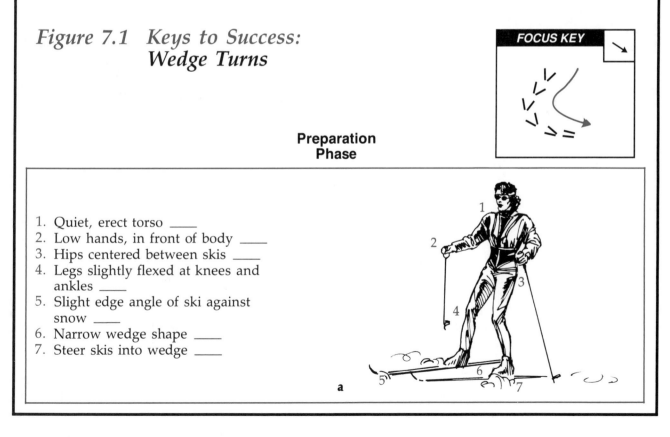

1. Quiet, erect torso ____
2. Low hands, in front of body ____
3. Hips centered between skis ____
4. Legs slightly flexed at knees and ankles ____
5. Slight edge angle of ski against snow ____
6. Narrow wedge shape ____
7. Steer skis into wedge ____

a

Execution
Phase

Part A

1. Torso remains quiet and erect ____
2. Hands remain low, in front of body ____
3. Hips remain centered ____
4. Legs extend slightly to raise body ____
5. Edge angle remains slight ____
6. Feet and legs twist in direction of turn ____
7. Maintain narrow wedge shape ____

Part B

1. Feet and legs continue to steer skis, particularly inside ski ____
2. Ankles flex slightly to lower the body and control turn ____

Transition
Phase

1. Feet and legs stop steering ____
2. Glide neutrally in wedge position ____
3. Prepare to steer in opposite direction ____

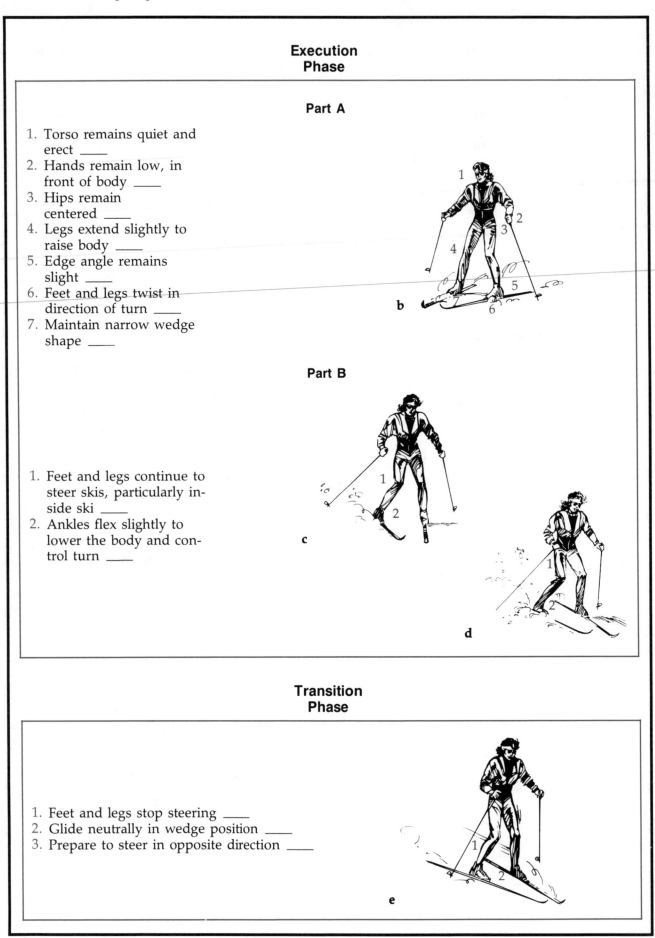

Detecting Errors in the Wedge Turn

Two major elements often contribute to problems with the wedge turn: the basic gliding wedge position and steering skills. You can't perform a wedge turn without a good wedge position, which can be overlooked if you rush the turn. Once you've examined your stance, analyze whether your steering involves the entire leg, which is necessary for effective turning. Also check whether you are incorrectly trying to steer by twisting your torso rather than your legs. Common errors with suggested corrections are noted in this section.

ERROR 🚫

CORRECTION

ERROR	CORRECTION
1. A wide wedge position creates excessive edging.	1. Raise your body by extending your legs, and use a higher stance. This reduces the width of the wedge, minimizes edging, and eliminates drag on the skis.
2. Your hips shift to the outside of the turn and actively transfer weight to the outside ski.	2. Keep your hips centered between the skis, which allows both the inside and the outside leg to steer the skis into the turn. The centered stance also better prepares you for the next turn.
3. Your torso leans to the inside or the outside of the turn.	3. Keep your torso quiet and upright above your lower body, which encourages the legs to steer the skis.
4. Your shoulders overrotate in the direction of travel, and your skis wash out.	4. Your shoulders are forcing the turn, by swiveling, rather than the legs performing the turn through steering. Your torso movement actually undermines the next turn.
5. You remain in a good wedge, and the turn never happens.	5. Your legs and feet are not steering the skis. Return to the steering drills in Step 1.

HOW TO EXECUTE THE STEP TURN

The step turn relies upon many small steps to move around the corner. It resembles the star turn practiced in Step 1, where your ski tails remain close together and the tips point apart as you step around a corner. But this is a star turn with a difference, because you are gliding throughout the move (see Figure 7.2, a-d).

Small steps are best to ride out the hill's momentum; glide on the outside ski for only a short time to enhance balance. These small steps also prevent you from crossing the tails of the skis, which can happen if you take a larger step sideways.

Keep your legs flexed at the ankle and knee to ride the gliding ski and absorb any changes in terrain. A stiff leg will cause you to lose balance quickly. This flexion also enhances your ability to push off the outside ski and step onto the inside ski securely.

If necessary, step from ski to ski slowly to regain your balance. As your skis come together in a parallel stance between steps, use that stable gliding phase to regain your balance before stepping again.

Use a very gentle grade to begin your practice, and begin the step turn where the hill flattens onto the run-out. Initiate the step turn earlier on the hill as you gain confidence.

Figure 7.2 Keys to Success: *Step Turns*

FOCUS KEY

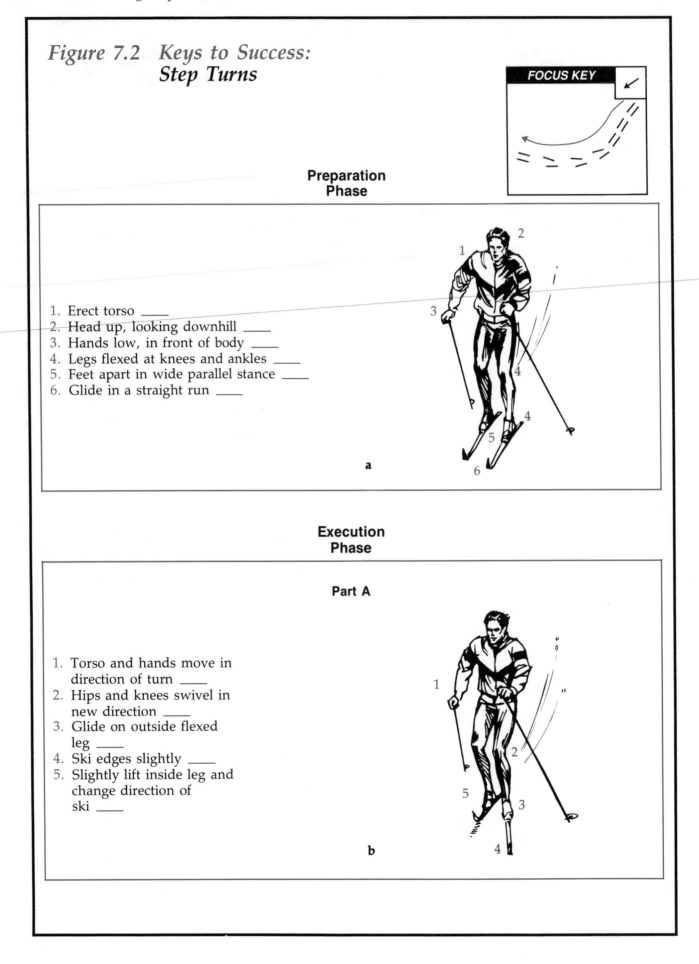

Preparation Phase

1. Erect torso ____
2. Head up, looking downhill ____
3. Hands low, in front of body ____
4. Legs flexed at knees and ankles ____
5. Feet apart in wide parallel stance ____
6. Glide in a straight run ____

a

Execution Phase

Part A

1. Torso and hands move in direction of turn ____
2. Hips and knees swivel in new direction ____
3. Glide on outside flexed leg ____
4. Ski edges slightly ____
5. Slightly lift inside leg and change direction of ski ____

b

Execution
Phase

Part B

1. Push off outside ski gently ____
2. Outside ski lifts off ground ____
3. Take small step sideways onto inside ski ____
4. Hands move in direction of turn ____

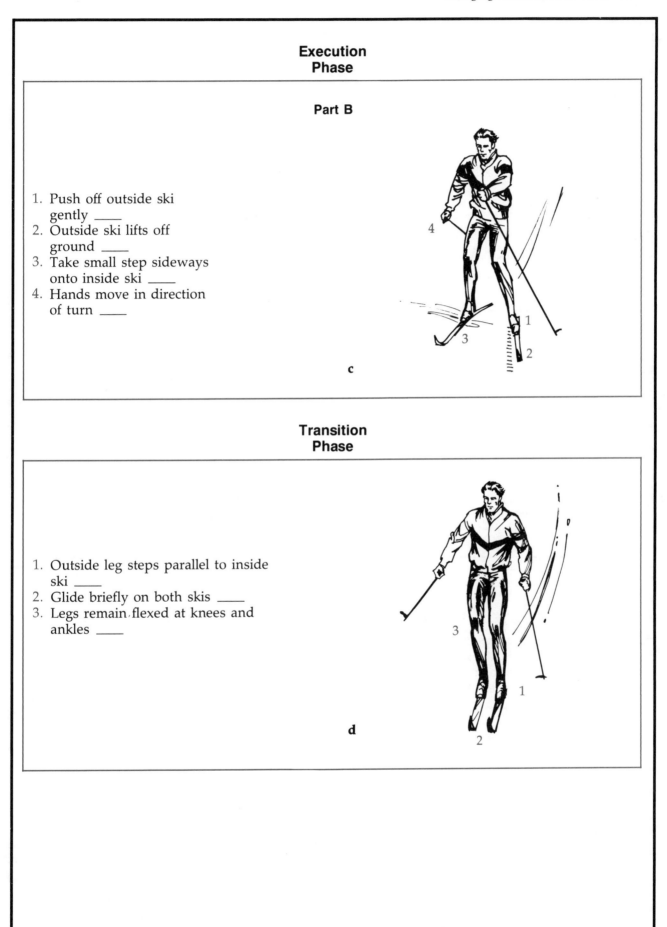

c

Transition
Phase

1. Outside leg steps parallel to inside ski ____
2. Glide briefly on both skis ____
3. Legs remain flexed at knees and ankles ____

d

Detecting Errors in a Step Turn

Discomfort with the step turn is often related to the steepness of the hill and the speed of your descent. Excessive momentum can undermine your comfort when you are gliding on the outside ski and interfere with stepping to the inside ski. Be willing to move to a gentler hill or descend from a lower position on the hill to reduce speed. Your increased comfort will allow you to balance on the gliding ski and concentrate on other elements in the turn, particularly the size of your step, which may be too large. Use the checklist in Figure 7.2 to analyze your performance.

ERROR 🚫

CORRECTION

ERROR	CORRECTION
1. The outside ski skids sideways, which prevents you from getting centered over the inside ski onto which you are stepping.	1. Take many small steps, and center your hips over the ski onto which you step. Glide on parallel skis between each small step as long as necessary to become centered and balanced over the skis.
2. A high stance sends your weight backward, which makes gliding on one ski difficult.	2. Bend at your ankles and knees to lower your stance and bring your weight forward. Keep your legs flexible.
3. Poor one-ski balance causes your weight transfer between the skis to be too quick.	3. Use the one-ski gliding exercises in Step 1 to improve your balance.

HOW TO EXECUTE A SKATE TURN

The skate turn is a more aggressive version of the step turn. The turn not only uses the hill's momentum but also can increase the speed at which you turn a corner. As a result, the basic elements are more dynamic than in the step turn.

The preparation phase remains the same: Approach the turn in a straight run. But the execution phase requires stronger edging, more aggressive pushing off from the outside ski, crisper weight transfer, and a diagonally forward step (see Figure 7.3a-d).

Flex your ankle and knee to push dynamically off the outside ski. Begin to move your body diagonally forward in the direction of the turn. Step forward around the corner, and move your weight onto your inside ski. Strong pushoff lets you move your hips forward to center them over the inside ski.

Double poling can be added to the skate turn to increase momentum. Pole over the outside ski, and recover your poles by swinging your arms forward over the inside ski after you push off. This extra forward momentum helps to center your hips over the new ski.

In its most aggressive form, the skate turn lets you rocket around a corner. When you push off the outside ski very dynamically, you can actually pop from ski to ski to increase momentum.

Figure 7.3 Keys to Success:
Skate Turns

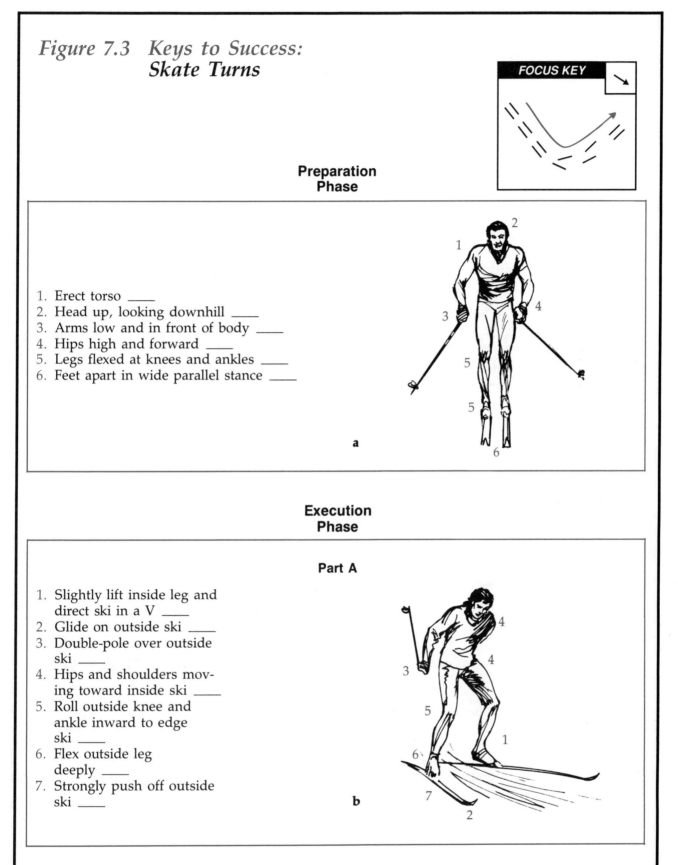

FOCUS KEY

**Preparation
Phase**

1. Erect torso ____
2. Head up, looking downhill ____
3. Arms low and in front of body ____
4. Hips high and forward ____
5. Legs flexed at knees and ankles ____
6. Feet apart in wide parallel stance ____

a

**Execution
Phase**

Part A

1. Slightly lift inside leg and direct ski in a V ____
2. Glide on outside ski ____
3. Double-pole over outside ski ____
4. Hips and shoulders moving toward inside ski ____
5. Roll outside knee and ankle inward to edge ski ____
6. Flex outside leg deeply ____
7. Strongly push off outside ski ____

b

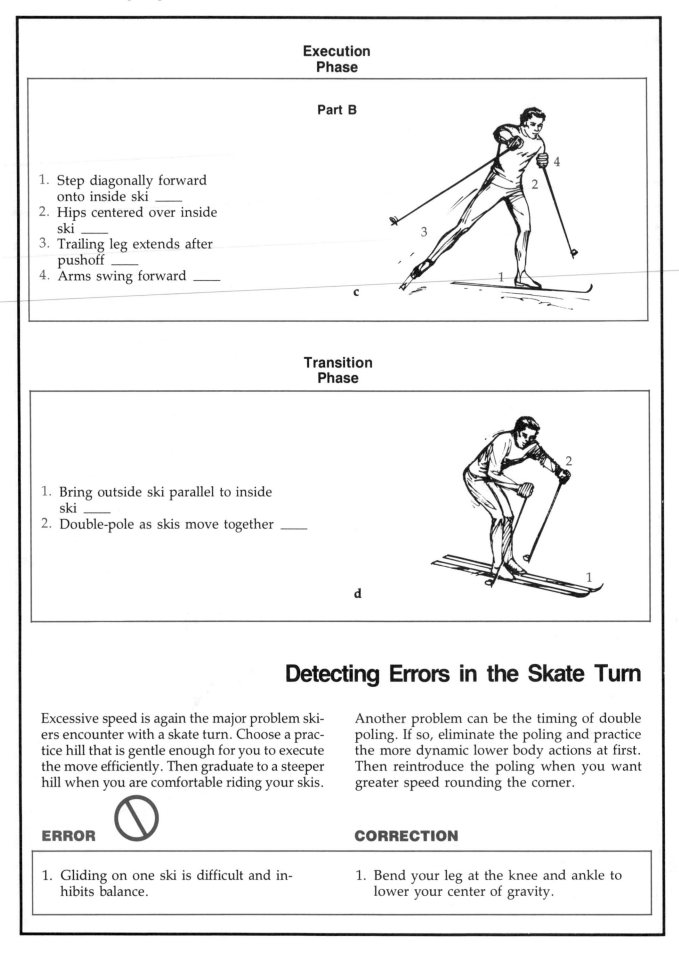

**Execution
Phase**

Part B

1. Step diagonally forward onto inside ski ____
2. Hips centered over inside ski ____
3. Trailing leg extends after pushoff ____
4. Arms swing forward ____

c

**Transition
Phase**

1. Bring outside ski parallel to inside ski ____
2. Double-pole as skis move together ____

d

Detecting Errors in the Skate Turn

Excessive speed is again the major problem skiers encounter with a skate turn. Choose a practice hill that is gentle enough for you to execute the move efficiently. Then graduate to a steeper hill when you are comfortable riding your skis.

Another problem can be the timing of double poling. If so, eliminate the poling and practice the more dynamic lower body actions at first. Then reintroduce the poling when you want greater speed rounding the corner.

ERROR 🚫

CORRECTION

ERROR	CORRECTION
1. Gliding on one ski is difficult and inhibits balance.	1. Bend your leg at the knee and ankle to lower your center of gravity.

	CORRECTION
2. Improper timing of the poling creates general awkwardness.	2. Pole over the outside ski, and swing the poles forward over the inside ski to center your body over it.
3. The outside ski overtakes or leads the inside ski and inhibits proper weight transfer.	3. Step diagonally forward onto the inside ski to let it lead the way around the corner.
4. The skis slap onto the snow rather than glide across it.	4. Swing the inside ski forward, low to the snow, and move your body forward with it. Don't lift your leg and step down onto the ski.

Changing Directions Drills

For your practice, choose a gentle hill that allows you to stay relaxed on your skis. A comfortable stance means your legs remain flexibly bent and can absorb the impact of any changes in terrain. The pitch of the hill should also allow you to glide on one ski with good balance.

If you feel wobbly with your balance, then select another hill with a gentler pitch. Now you can concentrate on practicing the new skills of steering, edging, and weight transfer in a more successful manner.

1. Partner-Push Wedge Turn Drill

Ask a partner to remove her or his skis and stand behind you between your skis. The partner pushes against your hips so that you glide across the snow in a stable position. (The partner should not push against the torso, or you'll bend forward at the waist.) When you sink into a narrow wedge position, steer both feet and knees in the direction in which you wish to turn. Your partner must be pushing hard enough to maintain your momentum throughout the turn.

When you want to turn in a new direction, return to a neutral wedge position that flattens your skis against the snow. This flattening releases the ski edges and prepares them for the next turn. Then begin to steer the other way by turning your feet and knees in the new direction.

With enough momentum, you can link several shallow turns on flat terrain. Strive for smooth directional changes by steering consistently through the turns.

Success Goal =

   a. 1 turn to the left with proper steering

   b. 1 turn to the right with proper steering

   c. 2 sets of linked turns

Your Score =

   a. (#) _____ turn to the left with proper steering

   b. (#) _____ turn to the right with proper steering

   c. (#) _____ linked turns

2. Fixed-Object Wedge Drill

Place a marker at the bottom of a gentle hill in one corner. Ski down the hill and turn toward the object by pointing your knees and toes toward the object. Your feet press against the sides of your boots nearest the object if you are steering strongly. Ski below the object, as close to it as possible.

Move the marker approximately 5 feet up the hill. Repeat the drill, and execute a sharper turn. Stronger steering is necessary.

Move the marker to the opposite side of the hill at the bottom. Repeat the foregoing steps to steer in a new direction.

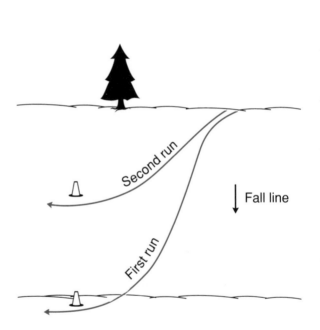

Success Goal = Steering the skis directly below each object

Your Score =

   a. (#) _____ feet from the first object on the left side of the hill

   b. (#) _____ feet from the second object

   c. (#) _____ feet from the first object on the right side of the hill

   d. (#) _____ feet from the second object

3. Poles Drill

Turn your palms toward the sky, and hold your poles horizontal to the ground as if you were carrying a tray. Keep the poles perpendicular to your knees and shoulders throughout the turn.

Descend the hill and steer the skis through the turn. As your knees swing around, the poles will also move toward the turning side. Turn to the other side.

Success Goal = 2 turns with the poles perpendicular to your body

Your Score = (#) _____ turns with poles held properly

4. Imaginary Basketball Drill

Pretend you are holding a basketball between your knees as you turn your skis. Point the basketball in the direction you want to go. The wide knee position keeps your skis flattened against the snow and reduces excessive edging.

Success Goal = 2 turns with knees apart

Your Score = (#) _____ turns with knees properly apart

5. Linked Wedge Turn Drill

Descend the hill, using shallow turns to change direction on the hill. On the first descent, simply steer your skis in gentle arcs to obtain a feel for the pitch of the hill. On the second descent, continue to steer your skis in a relaxed fashion, and count the number of turns during the descent. On the third descent, steer your skis more sharply in tighter turns and increase your number of turns.

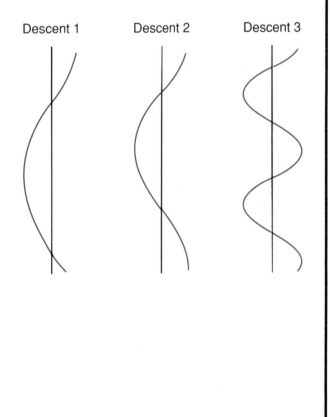

Descent 1   Descent 2   Descent 3

Success Goal = 3 descents with increasingly tighter linked turns

   a. 1 descent to practice linking turns

   b. 1 descent with shallow turns to count the number of turns

   c. 1 descent with sharper turns to increase the number of turns

Your Score =

   a. (#) _____ turns during first descent

   b. (#) _____ turns during second descent

   c. (#) _____ turns during third descent

6. Ski Slalom

Use a series of markers (poles, cones, plastic colored bowls) to establish a slalom course on the hill. Set the markers at least 10 feet apart in a straight line (if the hill is long and steep) to encourage longer, shallower turns. On a short hill, you may have room for only two or three markers.

   Turn around as many markers as possible on the descent (see Figure a). Negotiate the course until you can turn at each marker (see Figure b).

Success Goal = Turning around each slalom marker

Your Score = (#) _____ turns around
   (#) _____ total markers

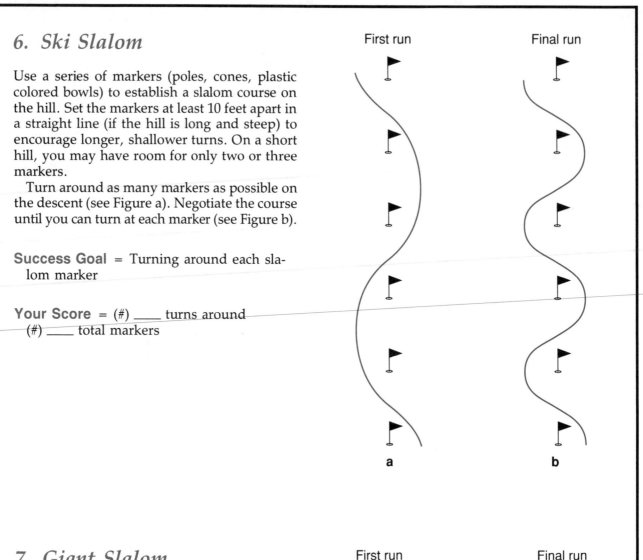

First run · Final run

a · b

7. Giant Slalom

Change the slalom course from a straight-line configuration to an offset course, where the markers are diagonally apart from each other. This offset configuration forces longer, deeper turns with stronger steering.

   Turn around as many markers as possible on the descent (see Figure a). Negotiate the course until you can turn around each marker (see Figure b).

Success Goal = Turning around each slalom marker

Your Score = (#) _____ turns around
   (#) _____ total markers

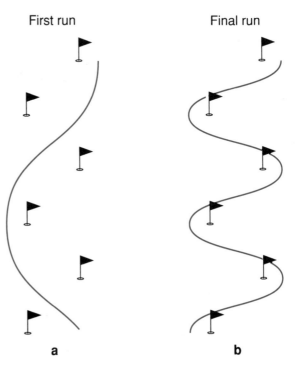

First run · Final run

a · b

8. *Fan Step-Turn Drill*

On flat terrain, execute a series of abbreviated star turns by taking small steps to one side, changing direction, and taking more small steps to the new side. Keep your steps small so that you stamp very narrow lines in the snow with your skis. When you finish, a scallop-shaped fan should appear in the snow. Practice until you complete a fan (without stepping on the tails of your skis at any point). If the tails do click together, your steps are too big.

Success Goal = 1 fan without stepping on the ski tails

Your Score = (#) _____ fan properly executed

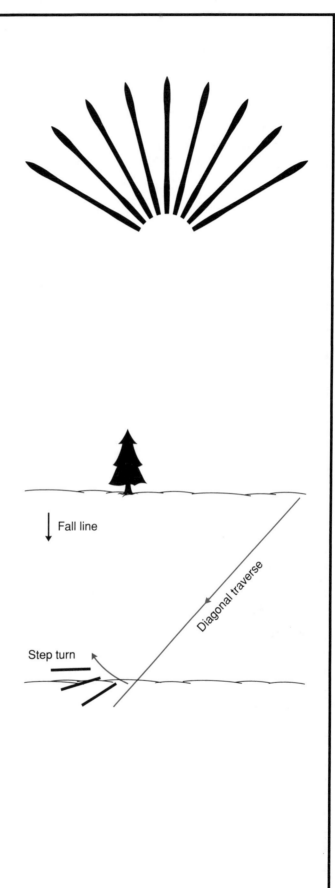

9. *On-the-Diagonal Step Turn*

On a very gentle hill, prepare to descend on a diagonal line from the top to the bottom of the hill. The diagonal route lets you ski across the fall line, which dampens your speed. Descend the hill in a relaxed gliding position. Begin to step sideways when your speed ebbs. Step toward the hill to continue to slow your speed.

Descend a second time and begin the step turn before your previous turn. You should be able to see your original path in the snow. The second turn requires that you step sideways when you are gliding more quickly. Be sure to keep your legs flexed to stay low and balanced while stepping. Repeat the step turn to this side until you can better your original route.

Then follow a diagonal route in the opposite direction, and repeat the steps in the exercise.

Success Goal = 2 improved step turns out of 4 turns

  a. 1 sharper step turn to the right

  b. 1 sharper step turn to the left

Your Score =

  a. (#) _____ feet earlier than original right step turn

  b. (#) _____ feet earlier than original left step turn

10. Touch-the-Pole Drill

On a gentle hill, plant a ski pole or slalom pole near the bottom of the hill (but on the hill rather than the run-out). Follow a diagonal traverse that ends approximately 5 feet below the pole, and execute a step turn. On the next descent, follow a route that ends about 2 feet below the pole, and finish with a step turn. On the next descents, execute tighter step turns that bring you closer to the downhill side of the pole. See if you can brush your shoulder against the pole.

Repeat the exercise to the other side.

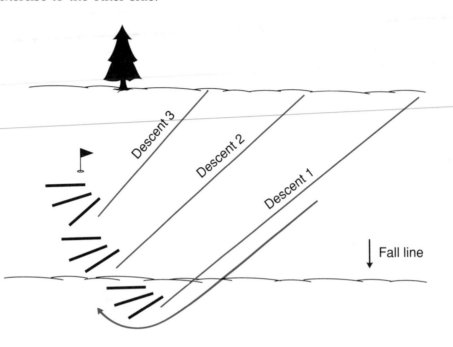

Success Goal = 2 improved step turns that are tighter to the pole

   a. 1 tighter step turn to the right

   b. 1 tighter step turn to the left

Your Score =

Right turn

   a. (#) ____ feet from the right pole during original run

   b. (#) ____ feet from the right pole during final run

Left turn

   a. (#) ____ feet from the left pole during original run

   b. (#) ____ feet from the right pole during final run

11. Through-the-Gates Drill

On the run-out below a gentle hill, plant two poles (or markers) 5 feet apart. Descend straight down the hill through the poles, and execute a step turn to either side right after the gates (see Figure a). Keep your legs flexed to handle the increased speed. Think of crouching through the move to lower your center of gravity and increase balance.

Move the poles to the bottom of the hill, where the pitch changes from incline to flat terrain (see Figure b). Repeat the exercise. Now you must step through the turn while gliding faster, which forces you to step more quickly. Keep moving the gates farther up the hill until you reach the point where you cannot turn immediately after the gates.

Repeat the exercise with step turns to the opposite side. Return the poles to the run-out to begin the exercise.

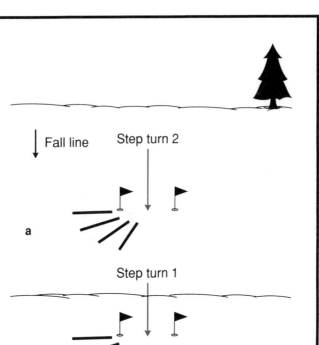

Success Goal = 2 faster step turns

a. 1 faster step turn to the right

b. 1 faster step turn to the left

Your Score =

Right turn

a. (#) _____ feet from marker in first turn

b. (#) _____ feet from marker in final turn

Left turn

a. (#) _____ feet from marker in first turn

b. (#) _____ feet from marker in final turn

12. Pop Drill

On flat terrain without poles, step quickly around a marker. Count the number of steps to turn completely around the marker. Then pop (spring) from ski to ski around the marker, and count the number of pops. Pop around again, using very bent legs to spring from ski to ski, and count the number of pops. As you push off more strongly, the size of your pops increases. You should be able to reduce the total number of pops each time. Repeat the exercise in the opposite direction.

Success Goal = A reduction in the number of pops during 3 turns

Your Score =

Right turn

a. (#) _____ number of steps

b. (#) _____ number of pops

c. (#) _____ number of pops

Left turn

a. (#) _____ number of steps

b. (#) _____ number of pops

c. (#) _____ number of pops

13. *Figure Eight*

Ski on flat terrain without poles along a figure-eight route, using skate turns to round the corners. Ski the course until you can round both corners with consistent speed and no stalling.

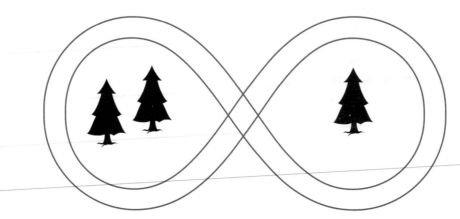

Success Goal = Skating a figure-eight course smoothly

Your Score = ____ Your sense: Was there smooth completion of a figure-eight course?

14. *Double Figure Eights*

Use the same figure-eight course where your route in the snow is clear. Ski the course once and count the number of skate turns used to complete the route. Now ski just outside the original route in a new figure-eight path, and count the number of skate turns. In the next circuit, reduce the number of skate turns to complete the course. Bend your legs to push off your skis strongly and get increased glide. See if you can complete the new circuit in the same number of skate turns used to negotiate the original route.

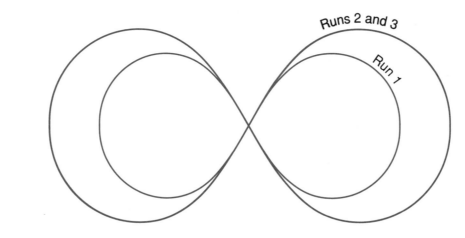

Success Goal = Improved skate turns with longer glide

Your Score =

a. (#) ____ skate turns to complete original route

b. (#) ____ skate turns to complete new route (first attempt)

c. (#) ____ skate turns to complete new route (second attempt)

15. *Tight-Corner Drill*

Plant a pole at the bottom of a gentle incline, and skate-turn in a gentle arc around the corner. With each successive run, execute the skate turns in a tighter manner until your path changes to a V shape. Make the legs of the V tighter and tighter. The path of your skis in the snow will create a visible V.

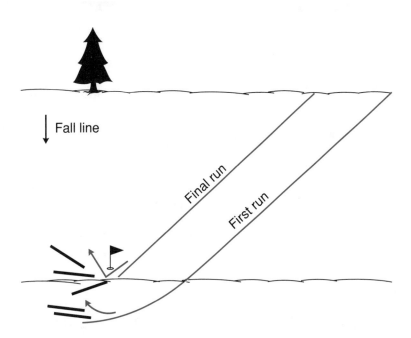

Success Goal = A V-shaped path around an obstacle

Your Score = ____ Your observation: Did you create a V-shaped path?

Changing Directions
Keys to Success Checklists

Ask your instructor, a coach, or a knowledgeable skier to observe your ability to change directions. Because balance is an integral part of these turning maneuvers, your observer should pay attention to your stance over the gliding ski(s). She or he can use the checklists in Figures 7.1 to 7.3 to evaluate your performance and provide corrective feedback.

Step 8 Developing Power in the Tracks

Handling the hills makes you a more confident skier familiar with the exhilaration of speed. When you return to the tracks, you're ready for more powerful moves that increase your speed on flat terrain. Two new maneuvers allow you to move more quickly: the kick double pole and the marathon skate.

The kick double, also known as the single-step double pole, is a variation on basic double poling. By using your leg for an additional push, you'll move faster than with the momentum generated by your arms alone. The marathon skate also uses a leg push, but in this case the ski is angled outside the track for the additional power.

Both moves rely upon efficient double poling. You will be more successful in learning the new moves if you already have fluid, powerful double poling, so you can concentrate on the new elements involved in the kick double pole and marathon skate.

WHY IS THE KICK DOUBLE POLE IMPORTANT?

When snow conditions or terrain make double poling too difficult, the kick double pole provides additional power. The extra power from the kicking leg supplements the power derived from double poling and enables you to glide farther. Skiers with limited strength in their arms benefit from the kick double pole. It takes more energy overall, but the results are greater.

The kick double pole uses your upper and lower bodies to create greater power, and like regular double poling it provides a good alternative to diagonal striding in the tracks. The maneuver stretches your muscles and relaxes them, particularly in the lower back, so that you can stride more comfortably and for a longer time.

The kick double pole is an important technique on flat terrain where irregular tracks may undermine balance. Gliding on two skis provides better stability, and the kicking action provides a strategic burst of power to ride up over bumps and rises in the tracks.

WHY IS THE MARATHON SKATE IMPORTANT?

Like the kick double pole, the marathon skate involves the entire body for greater momentum. But the angled ski, with its sharp inside edge pushing against the snow, actually provides greater power than the kick double pole, because the skating ski provides a better platform from which to push forward.

The marathon skate is a transitional move between classical and freestyle technique, because it uses elements of both types of skiing. The tracks provide direction and stability, and the skating leg provides power. The timing involved in the marathon skate is the basis for more advanced skating moves. Your practice here is important to your success with subsequent freestyle maneuvers.

If you are skating, the marathon skate allows you to ski in tracks with less damage to the grooming. This courtesy is appreciated by traditional skiers.

HOW TO EXECUTE THE KICK DOUBLE POLE

The ''kick'' in this move is actually like the pushoff in diagonal striding. You must push off the ski when your foot is under your torso in order to get good traction. As you push off the foot, the leg extends backward naturally and lifts the ski from the snow. At the same time, your arms extend forward in preparation to plant the poles in the double pole. Your body appears to open up from the waist, and it forms an extended diagonal line from the torso to this extended rear leg. At this point, you have pushed yourself onto your other ski, where you glide with your weight centered over your foot, which remains under your chest. Your hips should be forward, rather than back, where they would interrupt the smooth diagonal line of the body (see Figure 8.1, a and b).

Push against your poles to initiate the double poling, and let your torso compress to follow through. At the same time, your extended rear leg swings forward naturally. Your body appears to hinge at the waist, or close together, as your arms and leg approach your body. Complete the move by poling powerfully past your body. Your back will be parallel to the ground with complete torso compression (see Figure 8.1c). As you return your poles to the plant position, your body will naturally rise upward and prepare for the next move (see Figure 8.1d).

With a continuous kick double pole, the best strategy is alternating kicking legs to reduce fatigue. However, choose one leg during initial practice so that timing will be less confusing for you.

Figure 8.1 Keys to Success: Kick Double Pole

Preparation Phase

1. Front foot flat on ski ____
2. Rear foot prepares to push off ____
3. Torso bent forward slightly ____
4. Hands moving forward, past body ____
5. Ankles flexed ____

Execution Phase

Part A

1. Foot lifts after pushoff ____
2. Glide forward on straightened leg ____
3. Hands at shoulder level, ready to plant poles ____
4. Torso rises upward ____
5. Hips move forward, centered over ski ____

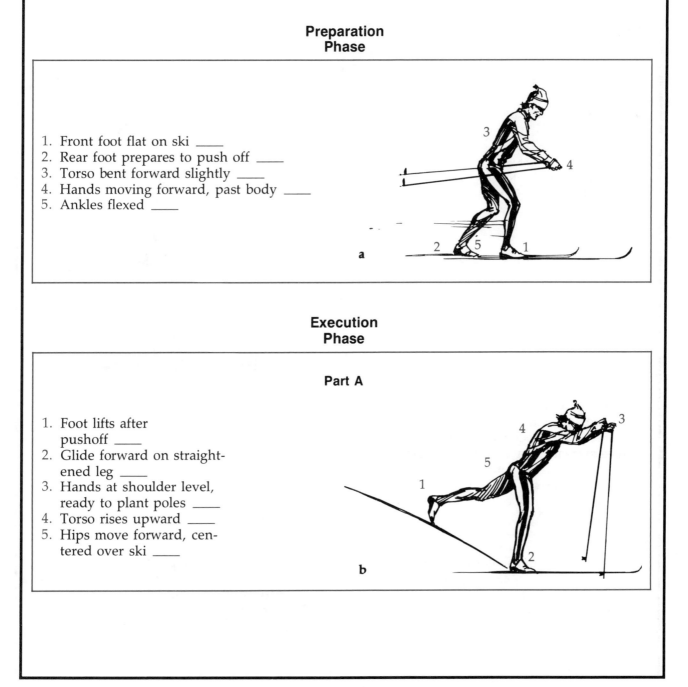

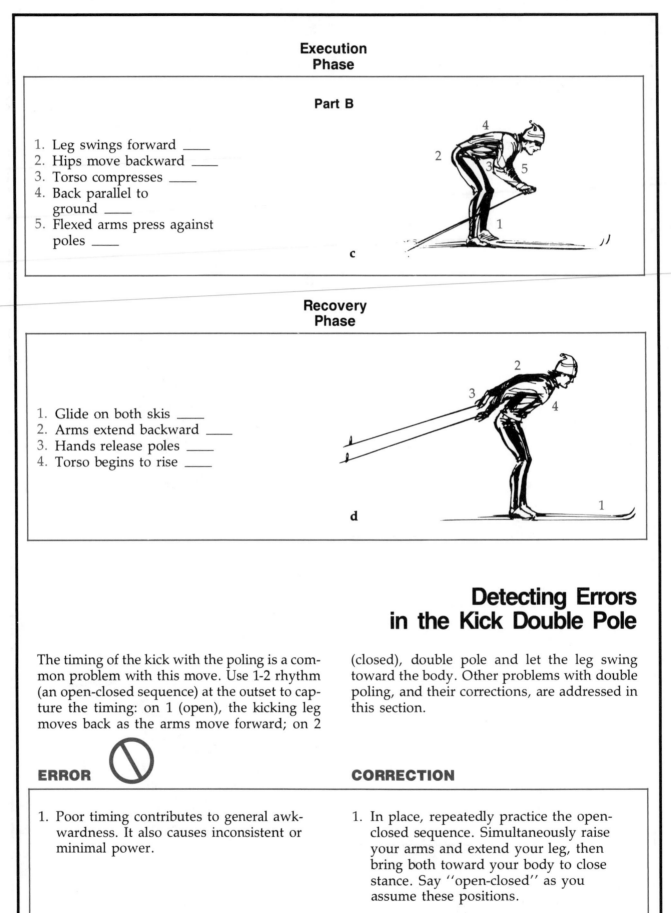

**Execution
Phase**

Part B

1. Leg swings forward ____
2. Hips move backward ____
3. Torso compresses ____
4. Back parallel to
   ground ____
5. Flexed arms press against
   poles ____

c

**Recovery
Phase**

1. Glide on both skis ____
2. Arms extend backward ____
3. Hands release poles ____
4. Torso begins to rise ____

d

Detecting Errors in the Kick Double Pole

The timing of the kick with the poling is a common problem with this move. Use 1-2 rhythm (an open-closed sequence) at the outset to capture the timing: on 1 (open), the kicking leg moves back as the arms move forward; on 2 (closed), double pole and let the leg swing toward the body. Other problems with double poling, and their corrections, are addressed in this section.

ERROR 🚫

CORRECTION

1. Poor timing contributes to general awkwardness. It also causes inconsistent or minimal power.

1. In place, repeatedly practice the open-closed sequence. Simultaneously raise your arms and extend your leg, then bring both toward your body to close stance. Say ''open-closed'' as you assume these positions.

ERROR	CORRECTION
2. Your kicking leg provides little power.	2. Eliminate the poling, and let your arms relax at your sides. Push yourself down the track by setting your wax when your feet are side by side, for good traction. Gently lift your arms every time you push off.
3. Your arms become fatigued.	3. Bent arms provide greater power than straight arms. Also check that you are compressing your torso. Begin the poling, and then bend at the waist to compress your torso.
4. You squat down when poling, because your legs have bent.	4. Raising and lowering your hips sends power down into the ground. Keep your gliding leg slightly flexed for good balance, without bending it repeatedly. Let your hips move forward and backward naturally with the poling rather than up and down.

HOW TO EXECUTE THE MARATHON SKATE

To begin the marathon skate, lift one ski from the tracks and angle it outward in a V shape. Keep your feet close together at the beginning of the skate. Because the gliding ski sits lower in the track, your skis will not touch.

Plant the poles for double poling in alignment with your tracked ski, but be careful to keep the pole tips behind the angled ski (see Figure 8.2a). Skiers commonly plant their poles between their legs in learning this move and fall forward over their poles.

Push down on the poles, and simultaneously step forward onto the angled (skating) ski. Your hips move slightly over the angled ski and shift weight to the skating ski. Let your double poling continue past your body (see Figure 8.2b).

Edge the skating ski and push off it strongly, pushing sideways and backward against the ski (see Figure 8.2c). The weight transfer between your skis should be crisp to quickly return your weight to the tracked (gliding) ski. Ride the tracked ski as you swing your arms forward and ready the poles for another sequence of marathon skating (see Figure 8.2d).

Use a wider V shape for a greater push, especially when you begin from a stationary position. The narrower V shape is effective for maintaining speed when gliding along. Once the timing feels comfortable, the double poling usually becomes more dynamic, with deeper upper body compression.

Figure 8.2 Keys to Success:
Marathon Skate

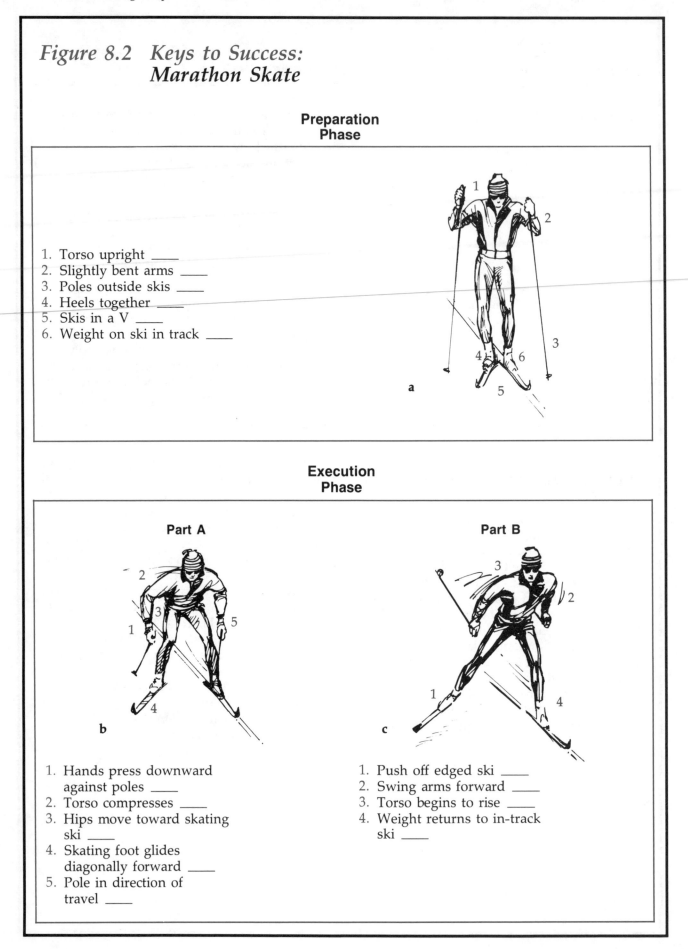

Preparation
Phase

1. Torso upright ____
2. Slightly bent arms ____
3. Poles outside skis ____
4. Heels together ____
5. Skis in a V ____
6. Weight on ski in track ____

a

Execution
Phase

Part A

b

Part B

c

1. Hands press downward
   against poles ____
2. Torso compresses ____
3. Hips move toward skating
   ski ____
4. Skating foot glides
   diagonally forward ____
5. Pole in direction of
   travel ____

1. Push off edged ski ____
2. Swing arms forward ____
3. Torso begins to rise ____
4. Weight returns to in-track
   ski ____

**Transition
Phase**

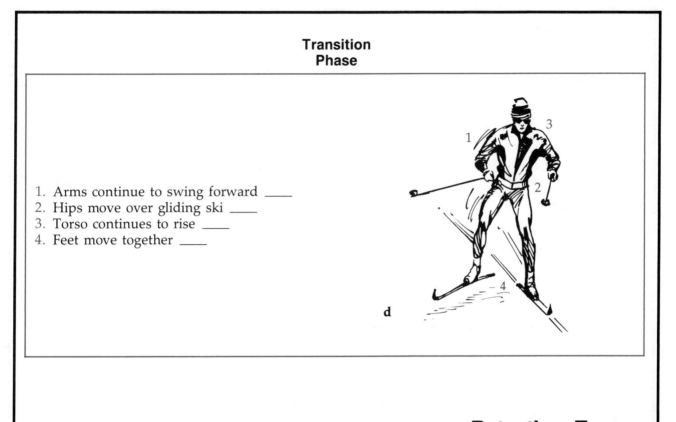

1. Arms continue to swing forward ____
2. Hips move over gliding ski ____
3. Torso continues to rise ____
4. Feet move together ____

Detecting Errors
in the Marathon Skate

As in the kick double pole, timing is a problem with the marathon skate. The poling and skating occur simultaneously. (At an advanced level, the poling is initiated a split second before the skating, but simultaneous timing is the best way to learn the move.) Transferring your weight can also cause problems, because it is a subtler action that requires commitment. Some skiers perform the marathon skate without weight transfer, not realizing they are working harder by compromising their ability to push off forcefully. Other errors and suggested corrections are listed in this section.

ERROR 🚫

CORRECTION

ERROR	CORRECTION
1. Poor timing and placement of the poling results in planting your poles between your legs.	1. In place, assume the skating position and plant the poles behind your skis. Push against the poles gently, and simultaneously step onto the skating ski. Move slowly down the track, poling and stepping at the same time.
2. You make no weight transfer, so you keep gliding continually on the ski in the track.	2. Shift weight onto the skating ski by moving your head, torso, and hips toward the ski. Lift the ski in the track slightly to test that the weight transfer is complete.

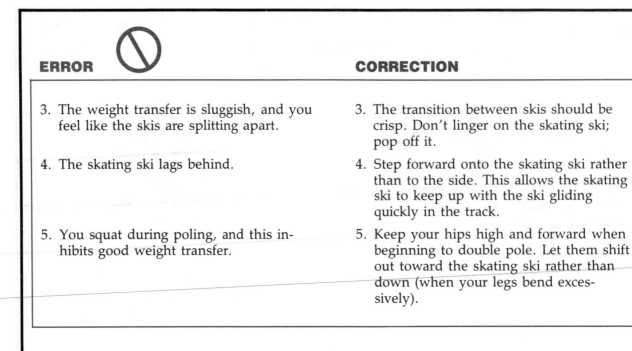

ERROR	CORRECTION
3. The weight transfer is sluggish, and you feel like the skis are splitting apart.	3. The transition between skis should be crisp. Don't linger on the skating ski; pop off it.
4. The skating ski lags behind.	4. Step forward onto the skating ski rather than to the side. This allows the skating ski to keep up with the ski gliding quickly in the track.
5. You squat during poling, and this inhibits good weight transfer.	5. Keep your hips high and forward when beginning to double pole. Let them shift out toward the skating ski rather than down (when your legs bend excessively).

Developing Power in the Tracks Drills

1. Open-Closed Drill

Use this drill in place to mimic the timing of the kick double pole. In the "open" position, extend your arms forward to begin poling (review Figure 8.1b). Hold the poles, but don't plant them; simply swing them back and forth. Also extend one leg backward off the snow. (Use the same leg each time.) Your arms and leg create a diagonal line along the length of your body in the open position. In the "closed" position, your arms pass your body and your leg returns next to the other leg (review Figure 8.1d).

Begin the exercise by slowly moving into the two positions. Think "open" (extended line of the body) and "closed" (hunched line of body). Increase the tempo, and say "open" and "closed" as you move into the positions. Repeat the drill with the other leg.

Success Goal = 40 correct repetitions of the open-closed sequence

    a. 20 correct repetitions with the right leg

    b. 20 correct repetitions with the left leg

Your Score =

    a. (#) _____ repetitions of the open-closed sequence (right leg)

    b. (#) _____ repetitions of the open-closed sequence (left leg)

2. *Alternating Open-Closed Drill*

Repeat the above exercise, but alternate the leg that extends rearward. You transfer your weight from ski to ski during the drill to accomplish this change.

Success Goal = 20 correct open-closed sequences with alternating rear legs

Your Score = (#) _____ repetitions of the open-closed sequence

3. *Single-Step Double-Pole Drill*

Stand in the tracks with your feet side by side and your arms relaxed at your sides. Step forward and, simultaneously, lift your arms into the plant position for double poling. You'll step onto the ski as your other leg naturally lifts off the snow. Double pole, and let your rear leg drift forward.
   Follow these steps gently without taking a big step forward or poling hard. This strategy will preserve the timing of the maneuver. If you lose the timing at any point, begin from a standstill to recapture it. Practice until you can ski a 50-yard stretch without losing the timing.

Success Goal = 50 yards of single-step double poling

Your Score = (#) _____ yards of single-step double poling

4. *Trust-Your-Partner Drill*

Without poles, stand facing another skier. You should be able to extend your arms forward and meet your partner's hands. Mimic the open-closed sequence again with alternating legs, but in the "open" position let your palms meet those of your partner (see Figures a and b). You should be able to brace against each other. Use opposite legs during this drill for better balance.
   After you become comfortable and rhythmic with the timing, begin to back farther away from

each other in 6-inch increments and repeat the drill until you achieve rhythmic sequences. It takes more and more commitment and trust to lean forward into your partner as you move farther away. Remember to bring your hips forward in the "open" phase and keep your feet flat on the skis. Don't let your heels lift off the skis, because this compromises balance. This drill promotes an aggressive kick double pole.

Success Goal = 2 changes in position, moving farther from your partner

Your Score =

    a. (#) _____ feet apart during initial practice

    b. (#) _____ feet apart after first change in position

    c. (#) _____ feet apart after second change in position

5. *Point A to Point B Kick Double Pole Drill*

Establish a 50-yard point-to-point course in the tracks. Count the number of kick double poles you use to complete the course. Now compress your torso deeply to improve the power in your double poling, and push off strongly to reduce the number of kick double poles during your second run.

Success Goal = A reduced number of kick double poles

Your Score =

    a. (#) _____ kick double poles during first run

    b. (#) _____ kick double poles during second run

6. *Over the Hump*

Choose a trail section that is relatively flat with a gentle, short hump in the middle. Double pole up to the hump. As you approach it, your speed will slow. Use kick double poles to boost your

momentum and carry you over the hump. Once you pick up speed on the other side, return to double poling or a straight run.

Count the number of kick double poles used to get to the other side. Then repeat the run and reduce the number of double poles. Strongly push off the kicking leg to increase your efficiency.

Success Goal = A reduced number of kick double poles

Your Score =

    a. (#) ____ kick double poles during first run

    b. (#) ____ kick double poles during second run

7. Longest Skate Push

Without poles and in the tracks, experiment with proper foot placement of your skating ski. Test two locations for your skating foot: behind the gliding foot and beside the gliding foot. Establish a starting point, and mark how far you can glide forward with each different placement. Begin with a behind-the-foot placement, and finish with side-by-side placement.

The best placement is side-by-side feet, because this keeps your body above your feet and your weight moving forward. Pushing from behind the gliding foot encourages your hips to drop back and counteract forward momentum. At an advanced level when you are gliding rapidly, your skating foot will actually land slightly ahead of your gliding foot.

Success Goal = Increased glide length from foot placement

Your Score =

    a. (#) ____ feet gliding with behind-the-foot placement

    b. (#) ____ feet gliding with side-by-side foot placement

8. Rocking Skate Scooters

Use a 50-yard course in the tracks, but leave your poles to one side. Use the angled, skating ski to push yourself down the track. Step forward onto the skating ski, transferring your weight onto it. Push off the skating ski to rock back onto the gliding ski. Aggressively rock your body back and forth over each ski to help get centered over it. Don't straddle your weight between your skis.

Success Goal = Active weight transfer from ski to ski

Your Score = ____ Your sense: Was there active weight transfer from ski to ski?

9. Three-Point Skate Drill

Use a 50-yard course in the tracks to practice the simultaneous timing of poling and skating in the marathon skate. Think of your two poles and the skating ski as three points of contact that land on the snow at the same time. Use a 1-2 rhythm: on 1, the three points hit the snow for you to pole and skate; on 2, you push off the skating ski and return to the gliding ski. Ski the course until the 1-2 rhythm feels consistent.

Change skating legs and repeat the exercise.

Success Goal = Smooth 1-2 timing

Your Score = _____ Your sense: Was there smooth 1-2 timing?

10. Tapping Drill

Ski down a 50-yard track using the marathon skate. When you shift your weight onto the skating ski, let the tracked ski lift gently off the snow. Let it tap the underside of your skating ski for half the distance to show that you have completely unweighted it. Then continue to unweight the tracked ski, but let it hover in the track without tapping the skating ski.

Success Goal = A transition from exaggerated to normal weight transfer

Your Score =

    a. (#) _____ yards of exaggerated weight transfer

    b. (#) _____ yards of normal weight transfer

11. Point A to Point B Marathon Skate Drill

Establish a 50-yard point-to-point course in the tracks. Marathon skate along the course, and count the number of marathon skates. Ski the course again, and increase your torso compression during double poling to decrease the number of marathon skates. Pushing strongly off the skating ski also propels you forward farther.

Success Goal = A decreased number of marathon skates

Your Score =

    a. (#) _____ marathon skates during first run

    b. (#) _____ marathon skates during second run

Developing Power in the Tracks
Keys to Success Checklists

Check your timing of the poling and leg push-off in the kick double pole and marathon skate. Make sure you are compressing your torso properly. It's important that an instructor, a coach, or a knowledgeable skier observe your performance of these more complex moves. He or she can use the checklists in Figures 8.1 and 8.2 to provide appropriate feedback.

Step 9   Uphill Diagonal Striding

As your skiing style becomes more dynamic, it's time to improve your transitions from flat terrain to the hills. Because your diagonal striding in flat or gently undulating tracks has become more fluid, you'll want to continue this rhythm as you approach steeper hills. Charging the hills in the diagonal stride will give you a heady feeling of accomplishment at this point in your development.

A crisply executed diagonal stride gives you enough traction to climb the hills smoothly, quickly, and, ultimately, with less energy than other moves. There is no need to change your strategy until the hill's steepness undermines the effectiveness of your diagonal stride and your strides begin to slip. Then you can switch to other alternative maneuvers for climbing, such as the herringbone, that you learned in Step 5.

WHY IS THE DIAGONAL STRIDE IMPORTANT ON HILLS?

The diagonal stride allows you to continue your gliding momentum up the hill, which gets you to the top quickly and efficiently. Because you ride the gliding ski, fewer steps are required than with other uphill maneuvers. Gone are the shorter, numerous steps of the herringbone; instead, the diagonal stride lets you cover the distance with fewer steps in less time.

You must aggressively transfer weight from ski to ski to stride up the hills; otherwise you cannot get enough traction from each ski to push off and move forward. Your development of crisp weight transfer means a transition from tentative to committed skiing. You must move strongly onto each ski and be centered over it to set your wax pocket and climb. The hill forces you to develop superior weight transfer skills that are an important step in your development as an advanced cross-country skier. When you return to flat tracks, you'll find that your diagonal stride is incredibly powerful with much longer glide.

You must have mastered the basics of the diagonal stride before proceeding with this practice. You need to transfer your weight properly between your skis without straddling between

them, which causes excessive shuffling in the tracks. You also must be moving your weight forward over your gliding ski rather than letting your hips hang back—this counterproductive position leaves your body behind and causes stalling and slipping on the hills.

HOW TO STRIDE UP THE HILLS

Choose a section of tracks where a flat stretch changes into a gradual but consistent uphill pitch. Avoid a hill that climbs too steeply and forces you to switch into a herringbone. You want to be able to continue the speed of your diagonal stride without a substantial change in the pace. Your tempo may change slightly as the length of your glide shortens at the steepest part of the hill near the top, but it shouldn't change dramatically. You want the hill to allow you to maintain a relatively consistent rhythm throughout your practice.

Aggressive lower body action is the key to hill climbing. Think of your spine as a column around which your hips and shoulders twist. As you stride up the hill, let your hips swivel fluidly to get longer glide. Your shoulders will twist more gently in the opposite direction while you pole.

With each stride, push your foot forward and keep your hips moving up and forward over the center of the ski. Let your hips twist around and forward, following the leg, to get an extra few inches from the stride. Don't let your hips get left behind, or you'll constantly have to drag this heavy weight up and over your feet to get good traction. Glide up onto your ski with the supporting leg in a flexed position, and stand firmly on your heel to help keep your hips forward (see Figure 9.1a).

As you prepare to shift your weight onto the new gliding ski, the trailing leg swings forward. Your hips must be forward as your feet come together, to get good traction at this point (see Figure 9.1b). Push off firmly, and glide forward (see Figure 9.1c).

The length of the poling matches the glide. As your glide shortens on the steepest pitch and turns into a running stride, the poling swing also shortens. Gradually increase the flex in your arms to create greater and quicker power. Continue to follow through with the poling behind your body, but decrease the degree of rearward arm extension. You'll naturally extend your arms in more fluid poling again as you reach the tip of the hill and lengthen your stride.

Some skiers lean forward too much from the waist in the mistaken impression that they are getting their weight forward over the skis. This position actually sends the hips backward and can cause ski slippage. There should be no break at the waist to interrupt the diagonal line of the body. Looking beyond the ski tips or at the top of the hill helps to tuck in the hips; it also allows the hips to rotate through the striding. The basic diagonal line of the body in relation to the terrain remains the same, whether you perform the move in flat tracks or on a hill (see Figure 9.1, a and c). However, you may *feel* as if you are standing more upright on the hill.

The foot of the gliding leg should always remain under you. Keep the angle between your shin and foot at about 90 degrees to allow your skeleton to support your weight (see Figure 9.1, a and c). Flex at the ankle slightly to get a powerful pushoff, but excessive bending at the ankle or knee when you glide or push off will fatigue you. It also makes your body bob, your momentum rising and falling vertically rather than forward into efficient glide.

Figure 9.1 Keys to Success: *Uphill Diagonal Stride*

Glide Phase

1. Head looks beyond ski tips ____
2. Front arm flexed ____
3. Hand moving past body ____
4. Torso projected forward, chest over gliding foot ____
5. Hip on gliding leg rotates forward ____
6. Straight shin on gliding leg ____
7. Foot flat, weight on heel ____
8. Rear leg extended ____

a

Pushoff Phase

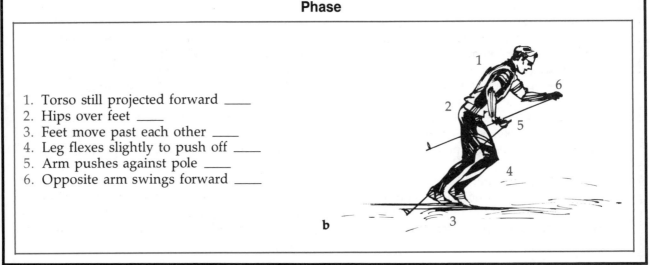

1. Torso still projected forward ____
2. Hips over feet ____
3. Feet move past each other ____
4. Leg flexes slightly to push off ____
5. Arm pushes against pole ____
6. Opposite arm swings forward ____

b

New-Glide Phase

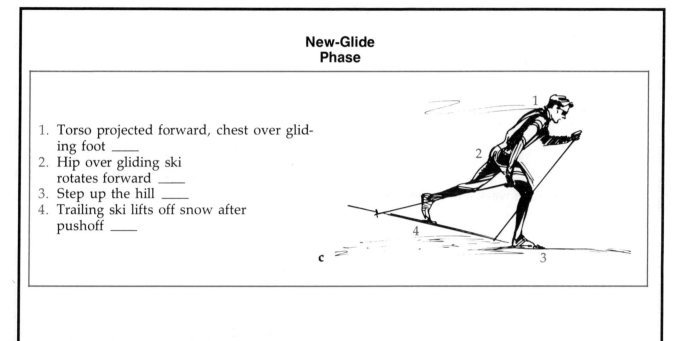

1. Torso projected forward, chest over gliding foot ____
2. Hip over gliding ski rotates forward ____
3. Step up the hill ____
4. Trailing ski lifts off snow after pushoff ____

Detecting Errors in the Uphill Diagonal Stride

Powerful use of the body, particularly the rotation of the hips around the spine, is important in striding up the hill. This hip swiveling, which sends the weight of your hips with your leg as it steps forward, promotes increased glide as you step up the hill. Also check whether a bent position of your upper body is inhibiting good lower body action. For more basic errors, also refer to pages 27 to 28 in Step 2.

ERROR 🚫

CORRECTION

1. Your gliding foot precedes your knee, which creates a backward angle with your shin. It also forces your hips backward and keeps your torso erect.

2. Your shin is bent excessively forward with a sharp flex at the ankle. Your hips may also rise and drop as a result, which creates bobbing.

3. Your hips remain tight or "blocked" with little or no rotation around your spine. Glide length is short.

1. The shin of the gliding leg remains relatively straight when you are riding the ski. Bring your knees and hips forward with the aid of an observer. Keep your chest over the gliding foot.

2. Straighten your leg until the shin forms a 90-degree angle with the foot. Raise your body slightly. Think of sliding your toes forward up the hill as you glide onto the ski.

3. Stand in place and exaggerate the hip rotation to loosen your spine. Then stride up the hill with exaggerated rotation. Think of pushing your ski uphill with a forward nudge from the pelvic bone.

ERROR	CORRECTION
4. Your skis slip as you move up the hill. Your pushing foot is too far behind your body to get good traction. Your body is hunched over.	4. Traction can be improved with better waxing, but you also need to move your hips forward and raise your torso to get your weight over your feet. This allows you to step up, up, up the hill.
5. Your poling feels weak and ineffective.	5. Slightly bend your arms for greater power, and push down and back with a pendular swing that ends behind your body.

Uphill Diagonal Stride Drills

1. Charge the Hill

Run up the hill with short strides, pumping your arms while you pole to maintain good timing. The quick tempo promotes good traction. Stomp the snow to set your wax if your skis slip. Look at the trail in front of your skis to help keep your hips forward. Glide downhill on a straight run.

Success Goal = 1 ascent with good traction

Your Score = (#) _____ ascent with good traction

2. Spine on a Line

Repeat the running charge of the hill, but emphasize the shift of your hips over each ski. This shift centers your spine (toe-knee-nose) over each gliding ski to improve balance and let you ride the ski longer. Pick a point at the top of the hill, ski straight toward it, and watch your head and body shift to each side of the landmark as you stride up the hill. Glide downhill in a straight run, shifting your hips over each ski.

Success Goal = 1 ascent with visible hip shift

Your Score = (#) _____ ascent with visible hip shift

3. Heel-Toe Drill

Ascend the hill with a running stride and count the number of strides. Now stride up the hill, sliding each foot forward so you glide on your heels. As the glide slackens, pretend to grab the snow with your toes to push off, and repeat the process on the other side. Count the number of strides during the run. This drill often increases your glide, reduces the number of strides, and slows the tempo slightly. Return to flat terrain with a straight run.

Success Goal = Fewer strides from first to second run

Your Score =

  a. (#) ____ strides during first run

  b. (#) ____ strides during second run

4. Swivel-Hips Drill

Stand in place and swivel your hips energetically to loosen them up. Then place your hands on your shoulders to minimize torso swivel and to isolate your lower body. Swivel your hips again. Carry this fluidity into your skiing.

    Stride up the hill, and exaggerate your hip rotation. Be uninhibited! Ask a partner to ski behind you and watch the back seam on your ski pants. The seam moves from side to side if you are rotating your hips properly. (See Spine on a Line.) Descend in a straight run, swiveling your hips slightly.

Success Goal = 1 ascent with visible hip rotation

Your Score = (#) ____ ascent with visible hip rotation

5. Timed Run

Stride up the hill in a relaxed fashion, and time the duration of the ascent. Descend in a straight run. Now time yourself striding up the hill with smooth hip rotation. A faster time should result. Be careful to use improved hip rotation rather than a quicker tempo to reach the top.

Success Goal = A quicker ascent from first to second run

Your Score =

  a. (#) ____ seconds for first run

  b. (#) ____ seconds for second run

6. Hill Bounding

Stride uphill, springing from ski to ski. The size of your forward step increases slightly and naturally, because you are pushing off a flexed leg. Glide on each ski as long as possible, and delay the return of the rear leg to eke out a few inches of additional glide. Descend in a straight run, bending and extending your ankles.

Success Goal = Stronger pushoff during the ascent

Your Score = ____ Your judgment: How strong is the pushoff?

7. Body Launches

Stride uphill in a springy fashion again, swinging each arm forward forcefully. Let the arm swing lead an aggressive launching of your body onto the gliding ski (the arm opposite the gliding leg swings forward). Your body mass hurtles forward onto the ski. Time the duration of your ascent, and compare it to your earlier times in Drill 5. Descend in a straight run.

Success Goal = A faster ascent of the hill than in Drill 5

Your Score = (#) ____ seconds for ascent

8. Glide-Stride-Glide Drill

Begin on the flat approach and ascend the hill, noticing the transition in your technique as the hill steepens. Your longer glide on the flat terrain changes to a shorter, choppier tempo on the steep section, before changing back to a longer glide at the top. Descend in a straight run.

Ask a partner to mark the two transition points. Now repeat the ascent and attempt to change your technique after the original markers. This drill forces you to improve your gliding ability through more forceful hip rotation. Let your body twist naturally without straining to improve your technique and pass the markers.

Success Goal = A change in the 2 transition points from the first to the second run

Your Score =

    a. (#) ____ feet after the first marker
    b. (#) ____ feet after the second marker

Uphill Diagonal Stride
Keys to Success Checklist

An efficient diagonal stride on the hills requires fluid, supple technique. When strain disappears from your movements, you find yourself climbing effortlessly uphill. Some improvements at this level can be very subtle. A trained observer can use the checklist in Figure 9.1 to provide you with valuable feedback about your performance.

Step 10 Telemark Turn Descents

Once you are comfortable with linked wedge turns on steeper hills, a challenging and exciting alternative is the telemark turn. As skiing's oldest turn, it is a curtsy-like move with a distinctive stance. The skier sinks into a bent-knee position where both skis create one long arc to carve the turn. The extended fore-and-aft position of the skis creates a stable turn well suited to a variety of ski conditions.

The telemark is a uniquely Nordic move, because the free-heeled nature of the equipment allows a skier to simply lift the rear heel and sink forward onto the leading ski in the telemark position. A cross-country skier can perform every Alpine turn as well, but the telemark is one of the most popular descents because of its uniqueness to cross-country skiing. For many skiers, this turn is an ultimate goal on the hills.

WHY IS THE TELEMARK TURN IMPORTANT?

The telemark turn is an elegant, enjoyable maneuver that is fun to learn because it is so different. The sensation of linking smooth telemark turns, with a distinctive raising and lowering of the body into the basic telemark stance, is a rewarding experience.

This turn gives you great versatility under many different snow conditions. You can vary the telemark from a long, slow turn in deeper snow to a sharp, dynamic turn on the packed trails of lift-serviced areas. It is also an especially functional turn for negotiating sharper corners on ski trails at cross-country ski areas and in ungroomed conditions on forest trails. While other turns provide good lateral stability, the telemark provides often-needed front-to-back stability.

HOW TO EXECUTE THE TELEMARK STANCE

Every telemark turn relies upon a basic telemark stance. Your successful execution of the telemark turn is based upon your body's ability to assume this stance. Most turning problems stem from a problem with the basic position.

From an upright stance, slide one ski forward slightly and step onto it with a bent leg. Let your opposite heel lift off the ski as you move forward. Lower your body until your front shin is angled forward and your trailing knee is near the front leg.

A moderate stance is appropriate for learning. Bend your legs enough to lower your center of gravity and feel stable. Let your body sink comfortably until your weight rests primarily upon your skeleton. Both legs will approach a near-90-degree-angle when bent. Avoid a very low stance that relies primarily upon muscle strength to hold the position, because this would tire you quickly during practice (see Figure 10.1).

Divide your weight equally between the front and back skis. Feel the weight resting on your flat front foot and on the ball of your rear foot. You must have weight upon the trailing ski to control its direction when moving. Keep your torso erect without bending at the waist to help center your weight between the skis. Tilting your pelvis slightly forward relieves any strain upon your back.

Although at first you may need to extend your hands to the side to help your balance, strive to bring your hands low and in front of your thighs. You can also hold the poles at midshaft as you practice the stance to be more aware of your hand motions.

Figure 10.1 Keys to Success:
The Telemark Stance

**Execution
Phase**

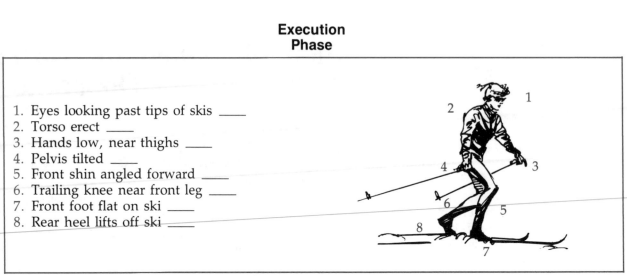

1. Eyes looking past tips of skis ____
2. Torso erect ____
3. Hands low, near thighs ____
4. Pelvis tilted ____
5. Front shin angled forward ____
6. Trailing knee near front leg ____
7. Front foot flat on ski ____
8. Rear heel lifts off ski ____

Detecting Errors
in the Telemark Stance

Correct leg position is crucial in the telemark. It is important at this stage to reinforce your leg position, because subsequent problems with telemark turns often stem from it. Common errors with the basic telemark stance are listed here with suggested corrections.

ERROR

CORRECTION

1. Your legs are split too far apart.

1. Bring the trailing knee forward until it nears the midcalf of your front leg.

2. Your knees are too close together, which places you in a crouched parallel position.

2. Move the trailing knee backward until it is aligned under your hip and shoulder. They form an almost straight line.

3. Your forward shin is angled backward. Your front foot leads the leg.

3. Move your front knee forward until it covers the foot.

4. Your torso hinges forward from the waist.

4. Stand upright, tilt the pelvis, and keep your posture perfect as you sink into the stance. Your shoulder, hips, and trailing knee form an almost straight line.

5. Your knees bow outward.

5. Sink into the telemark stance, and tuck your trailing knee toward the front leg.

HOW TO EXECUTE A TELEMARK TURN

A successful way to learn the turn is to begin from a very narrow gliding half wedge. Choose a gentle hill with a good run-out that allows you to coast comfortably to a stop; otherwise, you'll widen your skis into a braking wedge and have difficulty moving them into the telemark position.

Glide down the hill, and angle one ski into a half-wedge position (see Figure 10.2a). The angled ski will become the outside, or leading, ski. The straight ski will become the inside, or trailing, ski. Your straight-running ski remains flattened on the snow to let your skis glide together when you move into the telemark position (see Figure 10.2b).

Move forward onto the angled ski, which lifts your heel off the trailing ski. Then bend your legs to sink into the telemark stance (see Figure 10.2c). Initiate the turn by steering your feet and legs in the desired direction. Just like in the wedge turn, you push the big toe of your leading (outside) foot and the little toe of your trailing (inside) foot in the direction of the turn. Press

them against the sides of your boots to steer the front of your skis. Divide your weight equally between the skis so that you can control the pressure against the rear ski and steer it strongly.

Both knees aid the foot steering by also moving into the turn. The front knee leads the way, and the trailing knee follows closely. Don't let it lag behind and upset your balance. This rolling of your knees into the turn sets your skis on edge naturally, controls skidding, and helps to shape the turn.

Keep your hands low, and simply carry the poles without planting them. Finish the turn by smoothly returning to an upright position with both skis side by side. This stand-tall position prepares you for performing the next turn (see Figure 10.2d).

Use the entire length of the hill to link two turns. Make your first turn a shallow arc so that you can more easily change direction and steer into the new turn. After completing the steering in the first turn, raise your body and stand tall in a parallel stance before moving into a half wedge heading in the opposite direction. Bringing your feet close together in a narrow half wedge flattens your skis and allows you to change the leading ski for the next turn. Your skis change roles in this new turn. (The inside ski becomes the new outside ski.)

Slide the new lead (outside) ski forward, and sink into the telemark position. Let your skis glide closer together. Steer your feet and legs in the new direction. Rolling your knees into the turn sets the skis on edge again to control the shape of the turn.

On gentle terrain, your shoulders remain aligned with your body during the turn. But as the terrain steepens, your torso begins to move in opposition to your lower body. If your legs turn in one direction, your torso counters by twisting in the opposite direction. The goal is to keep your shoulders facing the fall line as much as possible to anticipate the next turn. Keep your upper body quiet to improve balance, and do most of the work with your lower body.

With practice, the small wedge in your telemark will disappear, and a fluid, advanced turn will result. You'll be able to execute the turn from a parallel stance and point your skis down the fall line on steeper hills. This transition occurs naturally after you develop controlled steering through your turns and comfort with the up-and-down movement between the turns.

A pole plant can aid the linking of quicker turns, but the longer cross-country poles can force you into a higher stance that forces you backward. Hold the poles below the grip for shorter turns, or use adjustable poles. Plant the pole as you rise up to initiate the new turn.

Figure 10.2 Keys to Success: Telemark Turn

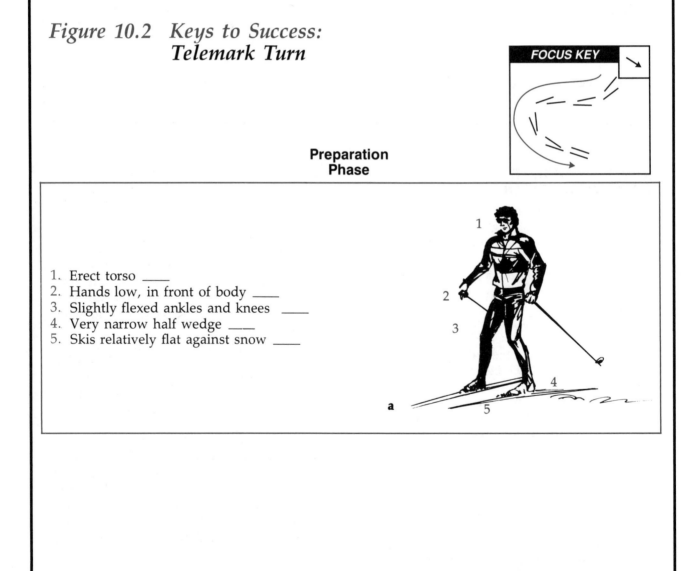

Preparation Phase

1. Erect torso ____
2. Hands low, in front of body ____
3. Slightly flexed ankles and knees ____
4. Very narrow half wedge ____
5. Skis relatively flat against snow ____

Execution
Phase

Part A

Part B

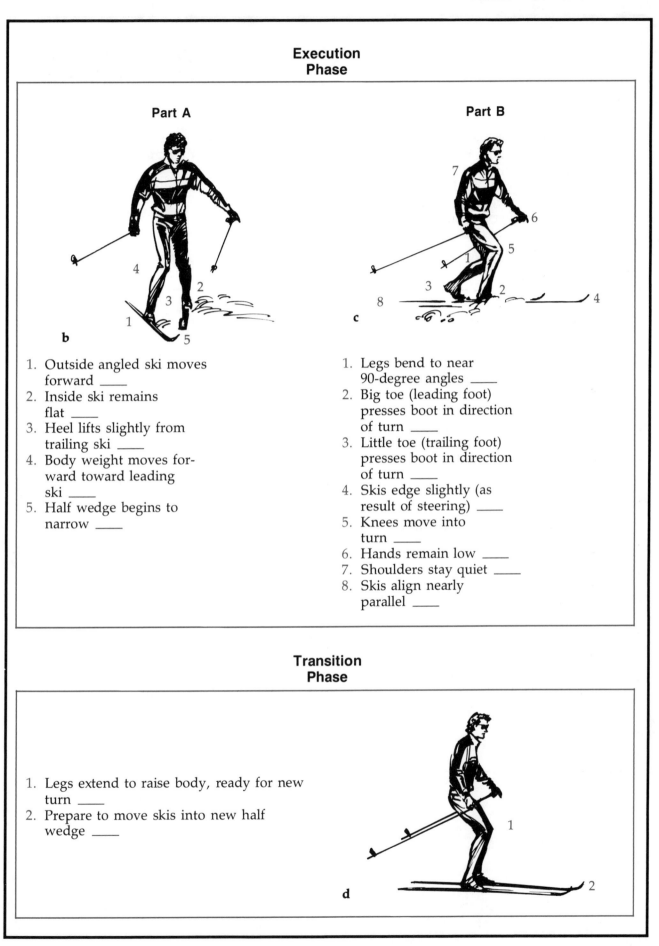

b

1. Outside angled ski moves forward ____
2. Inside ski remains flat ____
3. Heel lifts slightly from trailing ski ____
4. Body weight moves forward toward leading ski ____
5. Half wedge begins to narrow ____

c

1. Legs bend to near 90-degree angles ____
2. Big toe (leading foot) presses boot in direction of turn ____
3. Little toe (trailing foot) presses boot in direction of turn ____
4. Skis edge slightly (as result of steering) ____
5. Knees move into turn ____
6. Hands remain low ____
7. Shoulders stay quiet ____
8. Skis align nearly parallel ____

Transition
Phase

1. Legs extend to raise body, ready for new turn ____
2. Prepare to move skis into new half wedge ____

d

Detecting Errors in the Telemark Turn

First analyze your telemark position to determine if your basic stance is creating the problem. Use the "Detecting Errors in the Telemark Stance" section as your guide. Check to see if your wedge is too wide, which edges your skis too much. Then focus on your steering ability to see if both feet (particularly the inside foot) are steering the skis through the turn. Common errors and suggestions for improvement are listed here to help you solve problems with the telemark turn.

ERROR 🚫

CORRECTION

ERROR	CORRECTION
1. Your trailing ski crosses the tail of your leading ski.	1. Shift some weight off the leading ski to the trailing ski until you feel pressure on the ball of your trailing foot.
2. Your leading leg is extended and brakes against the snow.	2. Bend your leading leg and move your body forward until the knee on the leading ski covers the toes. This also flattens the leading ski and lets it skid and steer more easily.
3. Your arms stay high and wave.	3. Lower your arms and extend them to your sides if necessary to enhance balance. Eventually keep them quietly in front of your thighs.
4. Your basic stance is fine, but no turning happens.	4. Rotate your feet, knees, and hips to steer the skis in the direction of the turn.
5. The inside edge of your trailing ski catches on the snow.	5. Your skis are too far apart, in a braking wedge. Raise your body and begin the turn from a very narrow gliding wedge.
6. Your skis skid sharply and overturn into the hill.	6. Rotate your shoulders away from the hill, so they face down the fall line.
7. Your skis fail to come around into the second turn.	7. Raise your body to a neutral stance to eliminate the edging and flatten your skis against the snow. Sink into the telemark stance. Now begin to steer in the new direction.

Telemark Drills

1. Pole Test

Sink into the telemark position, and check your stance by lining up your ski pole with your trailing knee, hip, and shoulder. These body parts should be stacked almost on top of each other, if your torso is erect and your trailing knee is properly located. Repeat the test with the other side.

Success Goal = Proper telemark position

Your Score = (✓) ____ Proper telemark position

2. Telly Springs

In place, sink into a telemark position, gently spring up, and sink into a telemark position on the other side. As you change telemark positions, you can watch your body shift from one leading ski to the other to be centered over the ski. Ask another skier to check your stance, particularly the position of your legs.

Success Goal = 20 springs with correct telemark positions

Your Score = (#) ____ springs with correct telemark positions

3. Shuffle-Telemark Drill

Shuffle across flat terrain, and sink into the telemark position. Ride out the glide. Rise up, shuffle again, and sink into the telemark position on the other side. Use a cadence of shuffle-shuffle-sink. This rhythm will force you to alternate telemark positions.

Success Goal = 20 telemark stances without tipping

Your Score = (#) ____ telemark stances without tipping

4. Tandem Telemark Drill #1

On a gentle hill where you can coast to a stop, hold hands with a partner and begin your descent in a straight run. Then sink into the telemark position in unison, hold the position for 3 seconds, and smoothly rise up. Strive for a smooth transition from the low to the high position rather than abrupt up or down movement. A partner helps to provide lateral stability while you become comfortable with gliding in the telemark position.

Success Goal = 4 smoothly executed sequences

  a. 2 with left ski leading

  b. 2 with right ski leading

Your Score = (#) _____ smoothly executed sequences

5. Tandem Telemark Drill #2

Hold hands with a partner and glide down the hill in telemark position. Rise up and sink smoothly and slowly into the telemark. Alternate the leading ski each time. Count the number of times you assumed the telemark position during the first descent, and increase the number of times during the second run.

Success Goal = An increased number of transitions

Your Score =

  a. (#) _____ transitions during first run

  b. (#) _____ transitions during second run

6. Big-Toe Telemarks

Now glide down the hill alone, and lower yourself into the telemark position. Hold the position as long as it feels comfortable, and rise up smoothly to a standing position.

    On the next descent, sink into the telemark position and steer the leading ski around the corner. Press your big toe, knee, and hip in the direction of the turn to steer the ski. Also press the little toe of the trailing foot and the knee into the turn. This pressure allows the trailing ski to follow the arc of the leading ski through the turn.

    Repeat with a turn in the opposite direction. If you have difficulty turning to one side, reacquaint yourself in place with the sensation of big-toe pressure by pushing your toe (and ski) against the side of your ski pole.

Success Goal = A steered turn in both directions

Your Score =

  a. (#) _____ turn to the left

  b. (#) _____ turn to the right

7. Half-Wedge Telemark

Descend the hill linking half wedges. Head down the fall line, and make shallow turns. On the second run, add the telemark to the sequence.

Use a half wedge to begin turning. After the turn is initiated, move forward onto the angled (leading) ski, and lift your heel from the straight-running (trailing) ski. Sink into the telemark position, and steer with your foot and knee to complete the turn.

Rise up with your skis parallel, and move into a half wedge to initiate the next turn. Your skis switch roles. Your old trailing ski becomes the new angled (leading) ski, and the old leading ski becomes the new straight-running (trailing) ski. Sink into the new telemark position again to complete the turn.

As you become more comfortable linking the turns, your transition from the half wedge to the telemark will blend more smoothly. Rather than gliding in the half wedge, you can angle the leading ski and move onto it in the telemark position immediately. The half wedge will begin to disappear, and a pure telemark turn will emerge.

Success Goal = A linked telemark turn

Your Score = (#) ＿＿ linked telemark turn

8. Steep-Terrain Traverse

Rather than linking turns down the fall line of a steep hill, another strategy is traversing the hill (if it's wide enough) and executing a series of linked turns in one direction. A garland of consecutive turns, across the fall line and slightly up into the hill, helps you descend gradually.

Begin with a traverse where the uphill edges of both skis dig into the snow to prevent sideslipping. Sink into a telemark, using the downhill ski as the leading ski, and steer the skis slightly into the hill to reduce speed. Your knees move toward the hill. Rise up, move your knees slightly downhill to gently release the ski edges, and the skis begin to slide again in another traverse. Continue to turn into the hill to complete the descent.

If the hill is long enough, you can use a telemark turn to round the corner and repeat the exercise in the opposite direction.

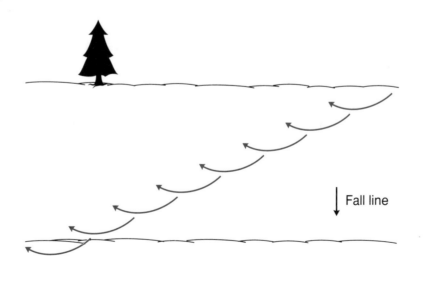

Fall line

Success Goal = A garland of telemark turns in two directions

Your Score =

   a. (#) _____ garlands to the right

   b. (#) _____ garlands to the left

9. Telemark Garlands With a Kick Turn

To descend a steep, narrow hill, you can also use telemark garlands to descend gradually. When you reach the edge of the trail, use a kick turn to change direction. Always turn your back to the hill to begin the kick turn, because if you fall, it's safer to fall backward into the hill.

From your traverse position, lift your downhill ski, turn it almost 180 degrees, and place it on its uphill edge against the snow. Plant both poles uphill of the skis for balance. Now lift your uphill ski, and turn it to match the other ski. You are ready to begin your telemark garlands in the opposite direction. Your route down the hill becomes a series of zigzags that gradually eat up the elevation.

Success Goal = A zigzag of garlands down the hill

Your Score = (#) _____ garlands

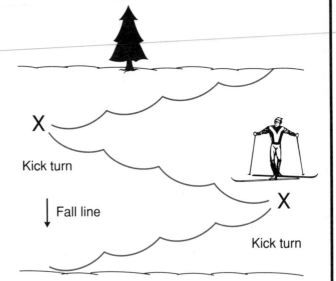

Telemark Turn
Keys to Success Checklists

Analyze the basic telemark stance for correctness at every point in your practice of telemark turns. An instructor, a coach, or a knowledgeable skier can use the checklist in Figure 10.1 to provide you with feedback about the stance. The checklist in Figure 10.2 provides the keys to evaluating and improving your telemark turn.

Step 11 **V-Skating Uphill**

Now that you are acquainted with climbing and descending steeper hills, you'll want to increase your ability to climb hills quickly and more powerfully. Skating the hills provides you with a fast way to the top. It's energy-intensive, but you can glide farther on your skis. In this section, you will learn how to climb hills more dynamically with different types of V-skating.

V-skating takes you out of the tracks and onto hard-packed snow. This "family" of maneuvers goes beyond the marathon skate, which is a half-skate motion. V-skating relies on a full skating motion, where both skis stay in a V shape for maximum power. Various forms of poling are added to further increase skiing speed.

These advanced skating moves are easier and more rewarding on skis free of kick wax. The ability to glide smoothly on the entire ski, without the wax pocket grabbing at the snow, lets you increase glide length. You can practice the moves on skis with a patterned wax pocket when the snow is hard and fast, but it's discouraging to practice on no-wax skis in new, abrasive snow.

WHY IS V-SKATING UPHILL IMPORTANT?

Cross-country racers discovered that V-skating was the fastest way to cover a point-to-point course. Because the techniques are significantly faster than classical maneuvers, two different types of races have evolved: classical and freestyle (skating). Now recreational skiers have discovered the exhilaration of speedier skiing through skating.

Both skis glide freely, even when edged, so there is no lag in the glide. The resulting speed is faster than any other maneuver on the same terrain. Skiers avoid the interruption of glide that occurs in diagonal striding when they set the wax to get good traction.

Skating lets you glide farther up the hill and gain extra inches with every step. As a result, you ascend the hill with fewer moves. Two maneuvers work well to skate uphill: the diagonal V and the V1 skate.

The diagonal V is an aggressive version of the gliding herringbone learned in Step 5. It works well on steep hills when V1-skating begins to stall. The alternate poling fills in the gap in power when the steepness cuts short the glide of the skis. V1, which refers to one double-poling action for every two skating steps, provides excellent power and longer glide on gentle to moderate hills.

HOW TO EXECUTE THE DIAGONAL V

Begin your practice at the base of the hill in the herringbone position (see Figure 11.1a). Take several steps up the hill with the herringbone to establish proper arm and leg timing.

Now shift your weight strongly from ski to ski, letting your hips rotate around to accentuate the movement. This loosening of the hips also allows them to stay centered over your feet and to move uphill with the ski (see Figure 11.1, b-e). It enables you to ride the gliding ski longer and to increase glide by several inches. But don't cut short the glide with a high tempo; prepare to take the next step up the hill only when the glide ebbs.

It's important to step aggressively up the hill to move away from the tail of the other ski (see Figure 11.1, b and d). A small step makes you step slightly sideways and promotes a wider, "straddled" stance to avoid stepping on the ski tails. You tend to waddle up the hill more slowly. Take a distinct step up the hill.

The steeper the hill, the greater the edging of the skis and the shorter the glide. However, the ski remains fairly flat on gentler sections with a little edging, and longer glide results.

At an advanced level, you can vary your poling with the steepness of the hill and bumps in the terrain. Your alternate poling may move toward a more "passgang" rhythm, where the arm and the leg on the same side provide momentum. This change happens naturally so it shouldn't be practiced.

Figure 11.1   Keys to Success: Diagonal V

Preparation Phase

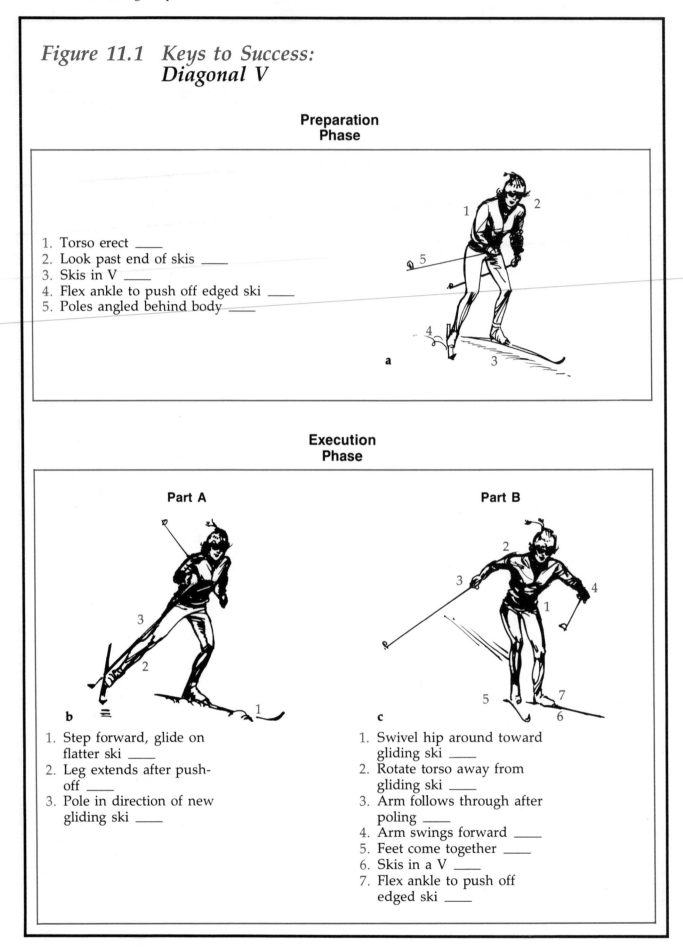

1. Torso erect ____
2. Look past end of skis ____
3. Skis in V ____
4. Flex ankle to push off edged ski ____
5. Poles angled behind body ____

Execution Phase

Part A

1. Step forward, glide on flatter ski ____
2. Leg extends after push-off ____
3. Pole in direction of new gliding ski ____

Part B

1. Swivel hip around toward gliding ski ____
2. Rotate torso away from gliding ski ____
3. Arm follows through after poling ____
4. Arm swings forward ____
5. Feet come together ____
6. Skis in a V ____
7. Flex ankle to push off edged ski ____

**Execution
Phase**

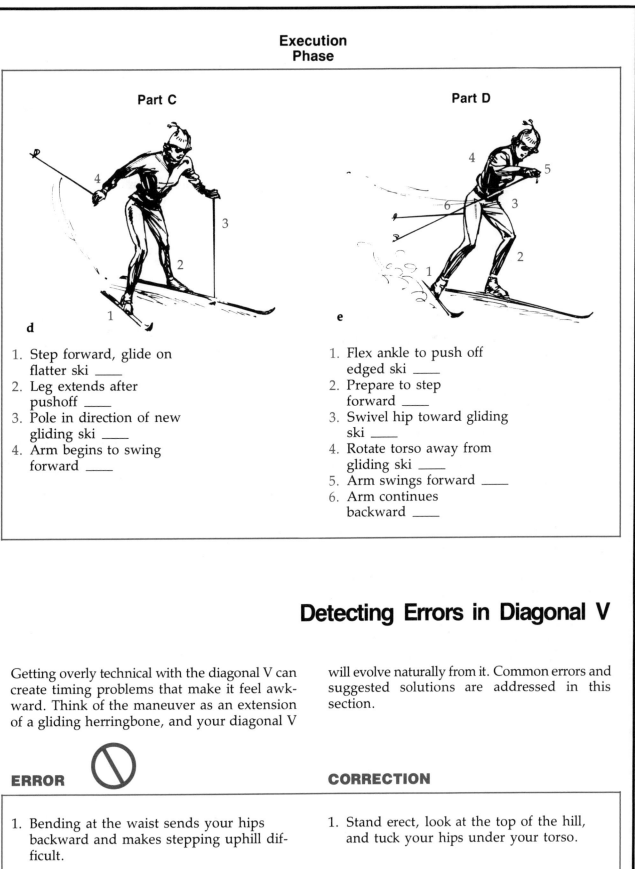

Part C

d

1. Step forward, glide on flatter ski ____
2. Leg extends after pushoff ____
3. Pole in direction of new gliding ski ____
4. Arm begins to swing forward ____

Part D

e

1. Flex ankle to push off edged ski ____
2. Prepare to step forward ____
3. Swivel hip toward gliding ski ____
4. Rotate torso away from gliding ski ____
5. Arm swings forward ____
6. Arm continues backward ____

Detecting Errors in Diagonal V

Getting overly technical with the diagonal V can create timing problems that make it feel awkward. Think of the maneuver as an extension of a gliding herringbone, and your diagonal V will evolve naturally from it. Common errors and suggested solutions are addressed in this section.

ERROR

CORRECTION

1. Bending at the waist sends your hips backward and makes stepping uphill difficult.

1. Stand erect, look at the top of the hill, and tuck your hips under your torso.

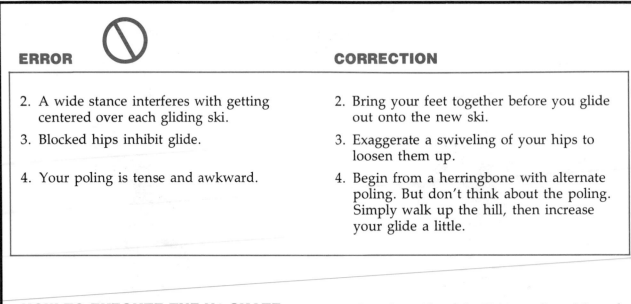

ERROR

2. A wide stance interferes with getting centered over each gliding ski.

3. Blocked hips inhibit glide.

4. Your poling is tense and awkward.

CORRECTION

2. Bring your feet together before you glide out onto the new ski.

3. Exaggerate a swiveling of your hips to loosen them up.

4. Begin from a herringbone with alternate poling. But don't think about the poling. Simply walk up the hill, then increase your glide a little.

HOW TO EXECUTE THE V1 SKATE

V1 requires that you double-pole once for every two skating steps you take. The side over which you pole is the ''poling'' side. The other side becomes the ''nonpoling'' side, where you simply skate with no poling.

Choose one side as your poling side, and plant the poles over it. Your hands will be slightly offset at the pole plant, as you keep the poles angled backward outside the skis (see Figure 11.2a). Double-pole over the ski, compressing with your torso for additional power (see 11.2b). Push your hands downward and behind your body for good poling follow-through (see Figure 11.2c). The return swing of your arms occurs over the nonpoling side, where it helps project your body onto the ski and center it over your foot (see Figure 11.2d). As the glide ebbs, return your hands to the poling side to initiate the sequence again (see Figure 11.2, e and f).

During poling, your hands follow a triangular path down one side of the V (poling side ski), up the other side of the V (nonpoling ski), and across the top to repeat the sequence.

It's important to keep your skis as flat on the snow as possible to reduce friction and enhance glide. As you prepare to push off each ski, swivel your body so it faces the new ski. Lean forward with your entire body. As you move away from the ski, it begins to edge naturally. Push off the ski and glide onto the new skating ski, which should be relatively flat on the snow.

Your learning will be more successful if you isolate each poling side during your practice. Complete the progression of drills for one side and then the other to reduce confusion, but spend an equal time poling with each side. Otherwise, a dominant poling side develops and undermines your ability to handle varying terrain. When a trail is uneven, skiers tend to pole on the high side of the trail and glide out on the lower side. You want to ski along the trail with the ability to switch power sides periodically to match the terrain and avoid fatigue.

Figure 11.2   Keys to Success: V1 Skate

Preparation Phase

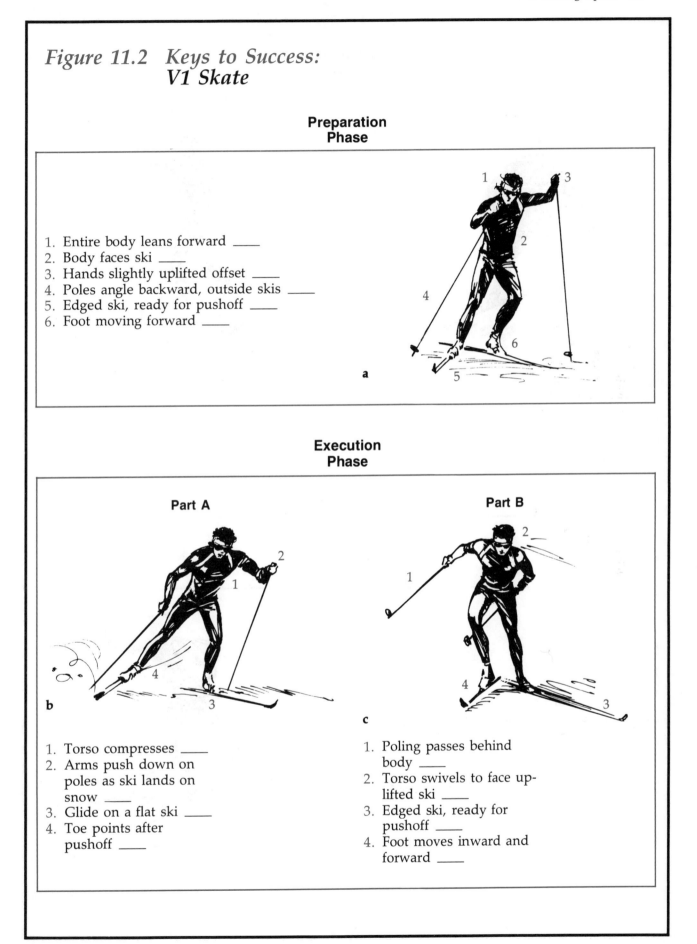

1. Entire body leans forward ____
2. Body faces ski ____
3. Hands slightly uplifted offset ____
4. Poles angle backward, outside skis ____
5. Edged ski, ready for pushoff ____
6. Foot moving forward ____

Execution Phase

Part A

1. Torso compresses ____
2. Arms push down on poles as ski lands on snow ____
3. Glide on a flat ski ____
4. Toe points after pushoff ____

Part B

1. Poling passes behind body ____
2. Torso swivels to face uplifted ski ____
3. Edged ski, ready for pushoff ____
4. Foot moves inward and forward ____

Execution
Phase

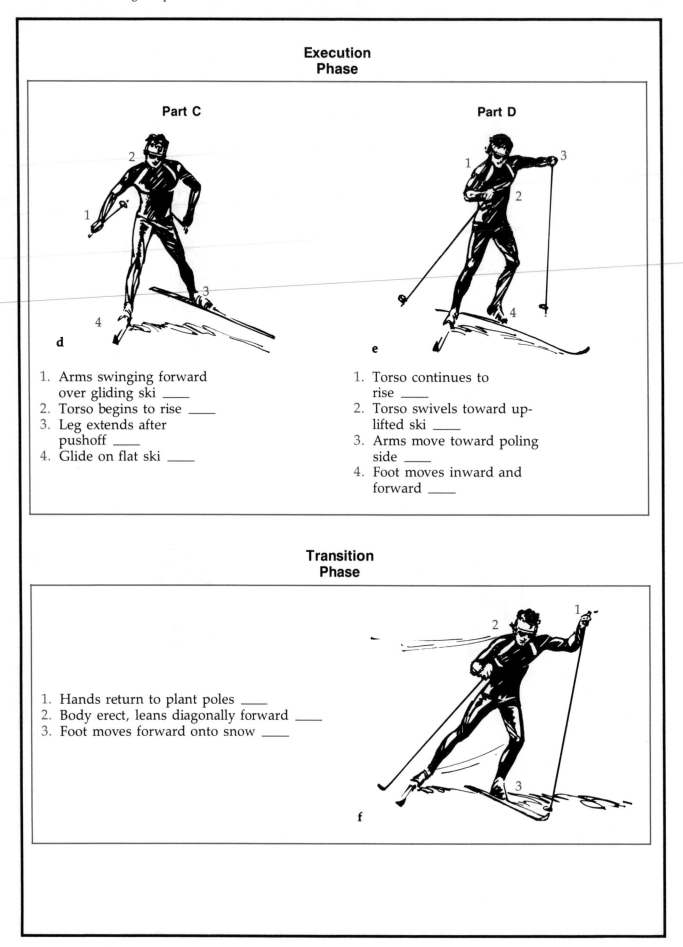

Part C

d

1. Arms swinging forward over gliding ski ____
2. Torso begins to rise ____
3. Leg extends after pushoff ____
4. Glide on flat ski ____

Part D

e

1. Torso continues to rise ____
2. Torso swivels toward up-lifted ski ____
3. Arms move toward poling side ____
4. Foot moves inward and forward ____

Transition
Phase

1. Hands return to plant poles ____
2. Body erect, leans diagonally forward ____
3. Foot moves forward onto snow ____

f

Detecting Errors in V1

The simultaneous timing of the poling and skating is an important part of V1. Problems with timing are usually a function of your comfort in gliding on one ski. With poor balance, you move too quickly from ski to ski and develop a high tempo. A review of the one-ski balance drills in Step 1 can be very beneficial at this point. Once you've focused on your timing, evaluate your performance for other improvements. Common problems and solutions are noted in this section.

ERROR

CORRECTION

1. You step early onto the ski without beginning the poling at the same time.

2. Your double poling uses little or no torso compression.

3. Your glide on the nonpoling side is very short.

4. Your feet fail to come together when you glide on one ski; a straddled stance and high tempo result.

5. You step down hard onto the new gliding ski; your leg may bend and straighten as you step down.

6. You squat down during the poling or let your hips drag behind your feet.

1. Simultaneously plant the poles and glide onto the ski. Synchronize your power forward.

2. Practice just the double poling, and bend fully at your waist to engage the large torso muscles.

3. Rotate your body to face the new skating ski, and move it completely over the ski. Align your toes, knees, and nose above the ski to center your body.

4. Push off strongly, and center your weight (especially hips) over each ski. Bring your heels together to tighten the stance and improve balance.

5. Swing your straight leg forward, and slide the ski across the snow as if you were scuffing gum off the underside. Don't lift it up; glide forward onto it.

6. Stand tall over each ski to move your hips forward and center your body over your feet.

V-Skating Uphill Drills

1. Gliding Herringbone-Diagonal V Drill

Stand at the bottom of a moderate hill, and begin to ascend the hill with the gliding herringbone. Strive for a relaxed execution with consistent motion to ascend the hill smoothly. Examine the width of your path.

Now climb the hill with more aggressive hip rotation. Swivel your hips from side to side to increase the glide slightly. An inch or two is fine; don't strive for too much glide, or you will strain the hip rotation. Examine your final tracks to discover how much you increased the width of the path through increased glide.

Success Goal = Improved glide in the diagonal V

Your Score =

   a. (#) _____ feet wide, original path

   b. (#) _____ inches of increased width in final path

2. Hip Rotation Drill

Ask a partner to ski behind you to provide you with feedback during this drill. Use more exaggerated hip rotation as you ascend the hill. Visualize the back seam of your pants as a central marker. Rotate your hips around with each step, and picture the seam shifting from side to side. Your partner can check whether the seam shifts away from the central position.

Success Goal = Visible hip rotation

Your Score = (✔) _____ Your partner's check of hip rotation

3. Close-the-Gap Drill

Ski about 10 feet behind another person, and mimic the diagonal V. Take bigger steps up the hill to close the gap between you. See how close you can get to the other person before the climb ends. Beware of flying ski poles, and keep a safe distance. Avoid tagging the other skier. This drill minimizes sideways stepping and reinforces uphill stepping.

Success Goal = Improved uphill step

Your Score =

   a. (#) _____ feet between skiers at beginning

   b. (#) _____ feet between skiers at end

4. No-Ski V1 Timing Drill

Remove your skis to learn the correct timing for V1 skating. Stand in place with your ski poles angled backward and planted comfortably in the snow. Your hands are usually level with your chin. The longer the poles, the farther the ski tips land behind your feet.

Remain in place for this drill. Begin with your arms at your sides and the poles trailing behind your body. Pick one foot to be your poling side, over which you will consistently pole. Lift your foot and arms, and drop them toward the snow at the same time. Then step onto the other foot. Step back onto the original foot, planting the poles simultaneously.

Use a 1-2 rhythm, and make sure that you have three points of contact (two poles, one foot) on 1. Once the rhythm is established, refine the move by ensuring that your hands are over your foot when you step onto it. Shifting your hands over the foot creates a noticeable difference in their position—the outside hand remains higher at the plant, and the inside hand rests lower.

Success Goal = 20 poling actions timed simultaneously with a step

Your Score = (#) _____ simultaneous poling/stepping actions

5. No-Ski Mock V1 Drill

Stand in place without skis, and prepare to step forward slightly as you pole. Repeat the 1-2 rhythm, with simultaneous poling as you step forward on 1 and another step forward without poling on 2. Walk along the snow for 20 yards to reinforce the proper timing.

Success Goal = Proper V1 timing while walking 20 yards

Your Score = _____ Your judgment: Is there proper V1 timing?

6. V1 From a Marathon Skate

Learning to V1 skate from a marathon skate is helpful. The timing of the marathon skate is the same as for V1, and the track guides your ski initially. This allows you to focus on combining the timing with gliding more comfortably. Use a section of tracks that fade into a groomed, untracked area where you can change into V1 technique.

Begin to marathon skate by stepping forward in the track at the same time as you double pole. This tracked ski is your poling side. Then transfer weight to skate onto your nonpoling side. Continue the sequence past the end of the tracks, when your poling-side ski will naturally move from a straight-forward alignment to a full skating angle like the other ski. Maintain the same 1-2 timing through the V1.

Success Goal = Proper timing in V1

Your Score = _____ Your judgment: Is there proper V1 timing?

7. Toe-Knee-Nose Drill

Begin with an in-place drill (with skis) to orient your body properly over the skis. Swivel your body so it faces in the direction of the step, and synchronize your poling and stepping. Align your nose and knee above your toes on the ski. Your hands and poles are also aligned parallel to the ski.

Now swivel your body in the direction of the nonpoling ski as you step (without poling) in this new direction. Let the poles swing across to be aligned with the nonpoling ski as you step in this direction, and swivel your body to face this new ski. Step on the new ski without poling. Simply align your hands over the ski on your nonpoling side to help center your body over the ski.

Repeat the drill until you feel your body rotate to face each ski prior to stepping. Centering your body completely over the ski enhances your ability to ride the gliding ski longer.

Success Goal = Toe-knee-nose alignment of the body over each ski

Your Score = _____ Your judgment: Is there proper alignment?

8. Heel-Click Drill

Your ability to skate onto each ski improves when you begin the motion from a tight stance with your heels together. This closed position provides you with stable balance and lets you swing your leg forward powerfully to skate onto the ski. Each time you push off, bring the foot near the new skating ski. Although you don't ordinarily click your heels together while V1-skating, try to do it to tighten your stance. Ski comfortably across flat terrain with a moderate tempo. Count how many times you can click your heels together over 25 yards. Repeat the exercise to beat your original total.

Success Goal = Heels close enough to click together while gliding on skating ski

Your Score =

    a. (#) ____ heel clicks during first run

    b. (#) ____ heel clicks during second run

9. Stand-Tall Drill

Standing tall on each ski helps to increase glide and speed, because your hips stay forward and centered. Stand tall during V1 at two important times: (a) just before double-poling over the poling side, and (b) as you raise your torso and recover the poles over the nonpoling side. Your body actually leans forward from the ankles to stand tall.

    Your hips will be far enough forward when you take the wrinkles out of your ski clothing across your groin. Ask a friend to ski alongside you on flat terrain and check whether you are far enough forward. Count the number of times in 25 yards that your suit is smoothed out. Repeat the exercise, raise your torso completely, and try to increase the number of times you are wrinkle-free while gliding.

Success Goal = Standing tall while gliding on skis

Your Score =

    a. (#) ____ wrinkle-free glides in first run

    b. (#) ____ wrinkle-free glides in second run

10. Quick-Change Drill

Once you have practiced the drills on each side, try to change poling sides while skiing. Walk through the change-up first. Choose a poling side, and walk across the snow, poling consistently on one side. The quick change forces you to pole on your original poling side and immediately pole again on the other side. If you begin by poling on your right side, the sequence becomes: pole (right)-skate-pole (right)-pole (left)-skate-pole (left). Your poling side has now changed, quickly enough to prevent a lag in momentum.

    To practice the quick change while gliding, ski at a relaxed pace on flat terrain or a gentle uphill to help you concentrate on the correct timing. Excessive speed can interfere with good timing. Ski until you have changed sides four times.

Success Goal = 4 quick changes

Your Score = (#) ____ quick changes

11. Waltzing-Change Drill

When you are gliding at higher speeds, a waltzing change-up works best to maintain good balance. Add an extra gliding step to the sequence to ride out the good glide, and then change to your new poling side. If you begin by poling on your right side, the sequence becomes: pole (right)-skate-skate-pole (left)-skate.

To practice the waltzing change, you need to have very good glide, or your momentum will die. Ski until you have changed sides four times.

Success Goal = 4 waltzing changes

Your Score = (#) _____ waltzing changes

12. Free Skiing With V1

Free skiing on a gentle uphill is the next step. If your skiing is strained or tense, then return to flat terrain and refocus on the preceding drills. If you can move consistently up the gentle hill without stalling, then you are ready for a steeper hill. Each time you increase the difficulty of the hill, analyze your actions in terms of the key skills in the exercises to continue developing good habits.

Success Goal = Smooth skiing uphill without stalling

Your Score = _____ Your judgment: Is there smooth skiing without stalling?

Diagonal V and V1
Keys to Success Checklists

Ask an instructor, a coach, or a knowledgeable skier to observe your skating maneuvers from a variety of vantage points. Your stance over the ski is best observed from the front, the size of your uphill step is more apparent from the side, and your hip rotation and weight transfer are more obvious from the rear. The observer can use the checklists in Figures 11.1 and 11.2 to evaluate your performance and assist with corrective solutions.

Step 12 Fine-Tuned Turning

If you are relaxed, comfortable, and balanced in your overall skiing, you can begin working on advanced turns. Skating is unusually effective in developing the ability to glide on one ski, so it lays a good foundation for advanced turning—you can direct and control your skis in a variety of situations, often with one leg acting independently of the other.

Advanced turns that we normally associate with Alpine skiers can be performed by cross-country skiers. The free-heeled nature of your equipment does keep you honest in performing the moves, because it tends to amplify any mistakes! But the rewards of advanced turns are great; they allow you to handle more diverse snow conditions with a greater variety of options.

Two turns allow cross-country skiers to handle steep terrain: the wedge christie and the parallel turn. Many skiers commonly use a wedge christie, often without knowing it. The wedge christie begins with a wedge but involves a parallel skid of the skis at some point in the turn. It leads naturally into a parallel turn, where the skis remain parallel throughout the turn.

WHY IS THE WEDGE CHRISTIE IMPORTANT?

The wedge christie allows you to initiate a turn quickly while effectively controlling your speed. It prevents the acceleration that can occur in a parallel turn when both skis are pointed down the fall line. You can increase or decrease the shape of the wedge before initiating the christie to make the move more comfortable and successful.

The wedge christie also provides lateral stability, which is especially helpful on steep or uneven terrain. The side-by-side position of the feet helps you maintain your balance while handling the faster speed of a steeper hill. Then you can move easily into a parallel stance later in the turn when you are ready to ride out or increase your momentum.

The wedge christie is a wonderful turn for negotiating the corners on steep trails. It enables you to slow down enough to get a feel for the hill and the corner, and then it allows you to carry your speed around the corner to continue the descent. Its skidded parallel nature reduces resistance against the legs and the resulting fa-

tigue that is common in gliding and braking wedges.

WHY IS THE PARALLEL TURN IMPORTANT?

Like the wedge christie, the parallel turn provides more lateral stability than the telemark turn. The side-by-side position of the feet makes it easier to handle faster, harder snow conditions. Cross-country skiers tend to use a wide stance—feet under the shoulders—to improve balance on advanced terrain. It is a good alternative to the telemark turn, which offers no lateral stability, particularly in icy conditions.

The parallel turn can be very effective on narrow trails, where space for turning is limited. Its execution is affected by snow conditions, however, and deeper, heavy snow can make turning difficult.

HOW TO EXECUTE A WEDGE CHRISTIE

On a moderate hill, initiate the turn with a narrow gliding wedge that involves minimal edging (see Figure 12.1a). Then raise your body slightly, by extending your legs, and stand tall on your skis. This vertical motion further flattens the skis against the snow (see Figure 12.1b). Steer both skis through the turn, and release the inside edge of the inside ski by rolling your ankle and knee toward the hill (see Figure 12.1c). Match it with the other ski in a parallel position. Then flex your legs slightly to lower your body and to increase your stability as you complete the turn (see Figure 12.1d).

Because your skis are relatively flat to the snow, they skid slightly through the parallel phase of the turn. Gentle edging shapes the turn and prevents overskidding. If your inside edge catches on the snow during the transition from wedge to parallel stance, your wedge position may be too wide. The wide stance forces the inside edges to brake against the snow. Remember to raise your body, which also narrows the wedge and flattens your skis against the snow. Then you should be able to slide the inside ski across the snow into position.

Where you turn in relation to the fall line is important to your mastery of the turn. At first, use the wedge to steer your skis through the fall line, which reduces the speed of the turn and increases your control. Move your skis into parallel alignment right when, or immediately after, you move through the fall line. With practice, you begin to realign the inside ski before the fall line and move into a parallel stance earlier in the turn. By this time, your comfort with carrying speed through the fall line will have increased, and the christie will occur much earlier.

Eliminate any poling during initial practice, because improper timing of the poling can interfere with proper execution of the turn. Later in your practice, introducing a pole plant can be helpful. The pole plant occurs as you rise up from the wedge; it acts as a signal to begin the transition to a parallel stance. Think "up-and-plant," then turn.

Today's longer poles can create some problems, because they can force you to stay too high or lift your arms excessively, which can send your weight backward. Grip the poles lower on the shaft during practice to encourage a low stance where necessary. The pole plant can also be modified from a more upright Alpine plant to an angled plant with the Nordic pole.

Figure 12.1 Keys to Success: Wedge Christie

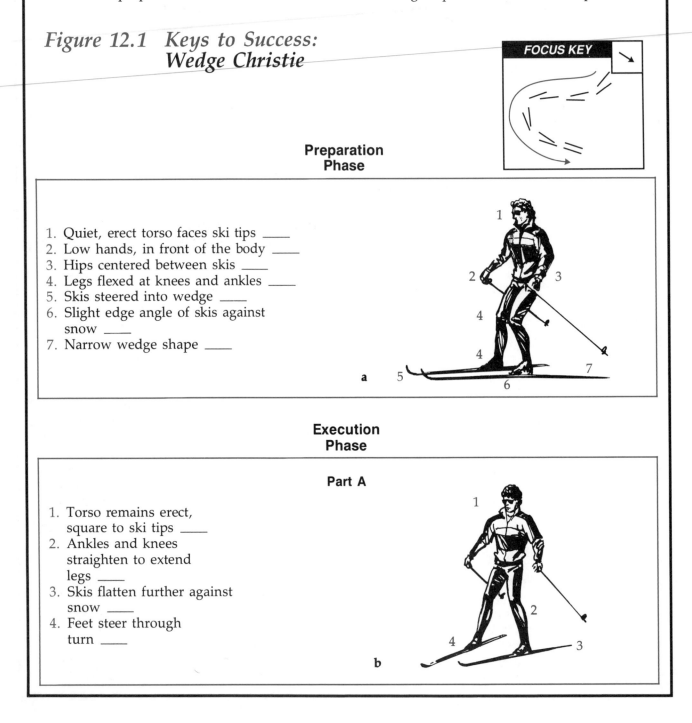

FOCUS KEY

Preparation Phase

1. Quiet, erect torso faces ski tips ____
2. Low hands, in front of the body ____
3. Hips centered between skis ____
4. Legs flexed at knees and ankles ____
5. Skis steered into wedge ____
6. Slight edge angle of skis against snow ____
7. Narrow wedge shape ____

Execution Phase

Part A

1. Torso remains erect, square to ski tips ____
2. Ankles and knees straighten to extend legs ____
3. Skis flatten further against snow ____
4. Feet steer through turn ____

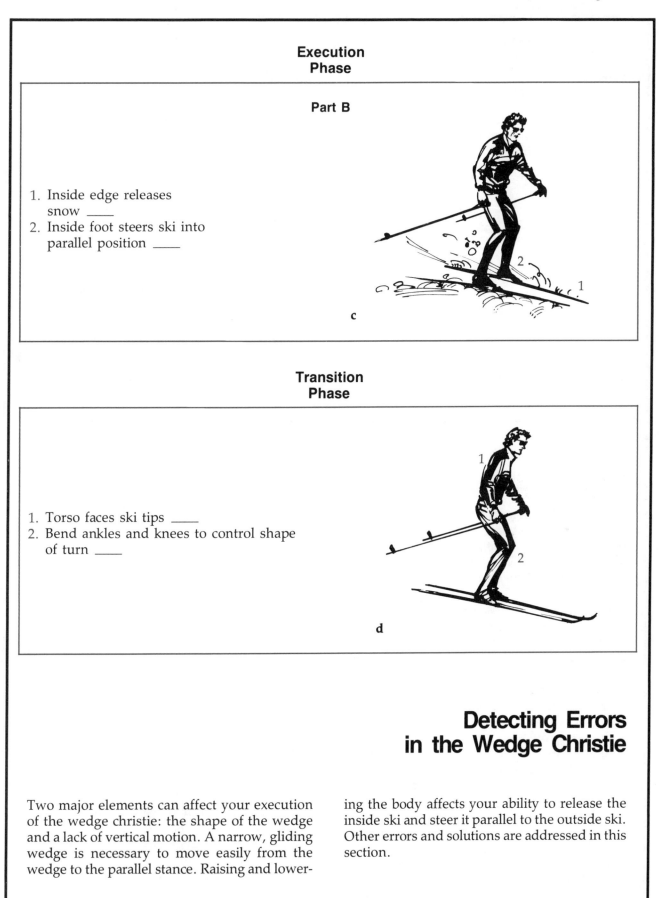

**Execution
Phase**

Part B

1. Inside edge releases
   snow ____
2. Inside foot steers ski into
   parallel position ____

c

**Transition
Phase**

1. Torso faces ski tips ____
2. Bend ankles and knees to control shape
   of turn ____

d

Detecting Errors
in the Wedge Christie

Two major elements can affect your execution of the wedge christie: the shape of the wedge and a lack of vertical motion. A narrow, gliding wedge is necessary to move easily from the wedge to the parallel stance. Raising and lower- ing the body affects your ability to release the inside ski and steer it parallel to the outside ski. Other errors and solutions are addressed in this section.

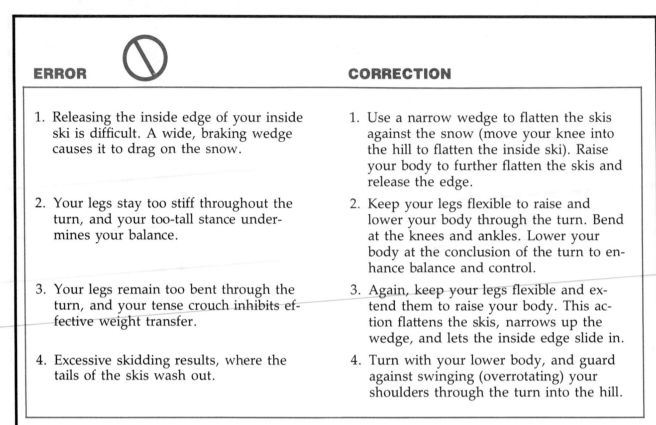

ERROR	CORRECTION
1. Releasing the inside edge of your inside ski is difficult. A wide, braking wedge causes it to drag on the snow.	1. Use a narrow wedge to flatten the skis against the snow (move your knee into the hill to flatten the inside ski). Raise your body to further flatten the skis and release the edge.
2. Your legs stay too stiff throughout the turn, and your too-tall stance undermines your balance.	2. Keep your legs flexible to raise and lower your body through the turn. Bend at the knees and ankles. Lower your body at the conclusion of the turn to enhance balance and control.
3. Your legs remain too bent through the turn, and your tense crouch inhibits effective weight transfer.	3. Again, keep your legs flexible and extend them to raise your body. This action flattens the skis, narrows up the wedge, and lets the inside edge slide in.
4. Excessive skidding results, where the tails of the skis wash out.	4. Turn with your lower body, and guard against swinging (overrotating) your shoulders through the turn into the hill.

HOW TO EXECUTE THE PARALLEL TURN

A wide, well-groomed hill works best for practice of the parallel turn. Choose a site free of bumps and ruts. A gentle to moderate pitch provides enough speed to help execute the move without too much speed to adversely affect balance.

The parallel turn evolves naturally from wedge christie practice. The ultimate goal is eliminating the wedge from the maneuver and keeping the skis parallel from beginning to end. Use a wide stance parallel position, where the skis remain as far apart as your hips (see Figure 12.2a). A narrower stance with ankles close together will inhibit balance.

Both legs must independently rotate the skis into the parallel turn for the steering to be effective. If the outside ski does most of the work, the inside ski gets left behind or provides little support. Let the inside knee and foot lead the steering and point in the direction of the turn. This strategy will make turning easier and will help eliminate the wedge.

Again, obvious vertical motion aids the parallel turn. Raise your body upward and forward down the hill by extending your legs (see Figure 12.2, a and b). This action releases pressure against the skis and helps to initiate the steering (see Figure 12.2c). Lower your body to control edging as you finish the turn (see Figure 12.d). The key to vertical motion is flexing at the *ankles* as well as the knees and avoiding excessive bending at the waist.

On steeper terrain, the upper body acts independently of the lower body just like in the advanced telemark turn. Twist your torso away from the direction of your legs toward the fall line to prevent overturning. This countering of the torso also readies you for the next turn. It keeps your upper body oriented down the fall line to help execute quicker turns.

The more your knees drive into the hill to turn on steep terrain, the more you want to offset this action by also leaning your torso down the hill. Your body becomes angulated along its length to maintain balance.

Poling can make the parallel turn more dynamic. Again, you may want to hold the shaft below the grip during initial practice, because cross-country's longer poles create a high-hands position that can interfere with good balance. You can also angle the longer pole slightly as you plant rather than use an Alpine-style upright plant.

Use the pole plant as you raise your body in preparation for steering the skis (see Figure 12.2a). Touch the snow lightly with your downhill pole, and turn around it. If the timing is awkward, eliminate the poles and concentrate on the mechanics of the turn, which should spring from your body anyway.

Figure 12.2 Keys to Success: Parallel Turn

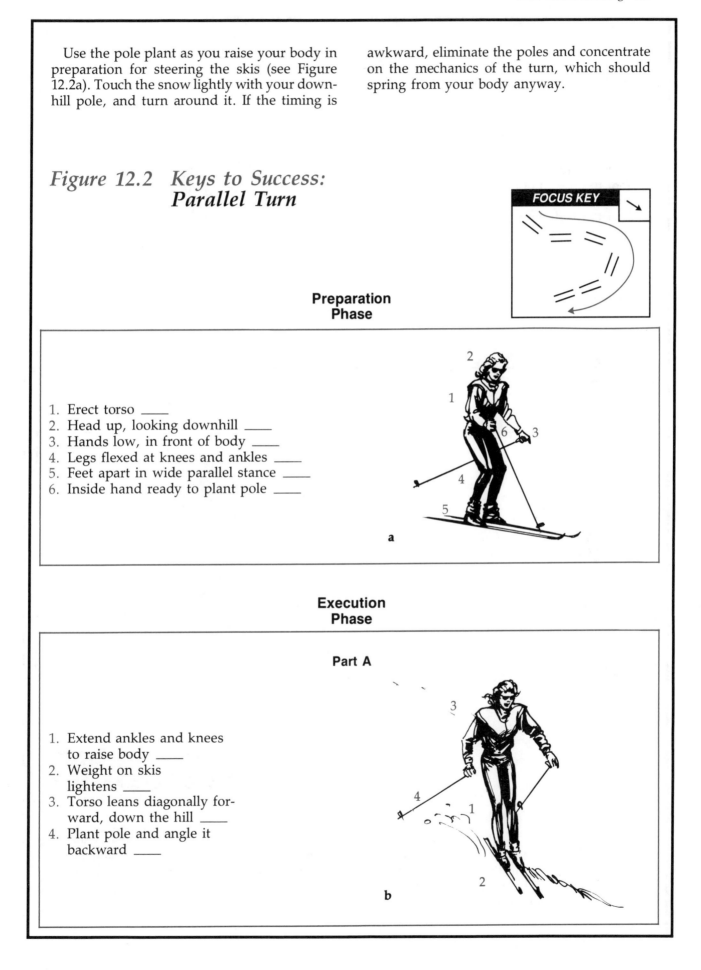

Preparation Phase

FOCUS KEY

1. Erect torso ____
2. Head up, looking downhill ____
3. Hands low, in front of body ____
4. Legs flexed at knees and ankles ____
5. Feet apart in wide parallel stance ____
6. Inside hand ready to plant pole ____

a

Execution Phase

Part A

1. Extend ankles and knees to raise body ____
2. Weight on skis lightens ____
3. Torso leans diagonally forward, down the hill ____
4. Plant pole and angle it backward ____

b

Execution
Phase

Part B

1. Twist inside knee and foot in direction of turn ____
2. Twist outside knee and foot in direction of turn ____
3. Uphill ski leads slightly ____
4. Skis skid ____

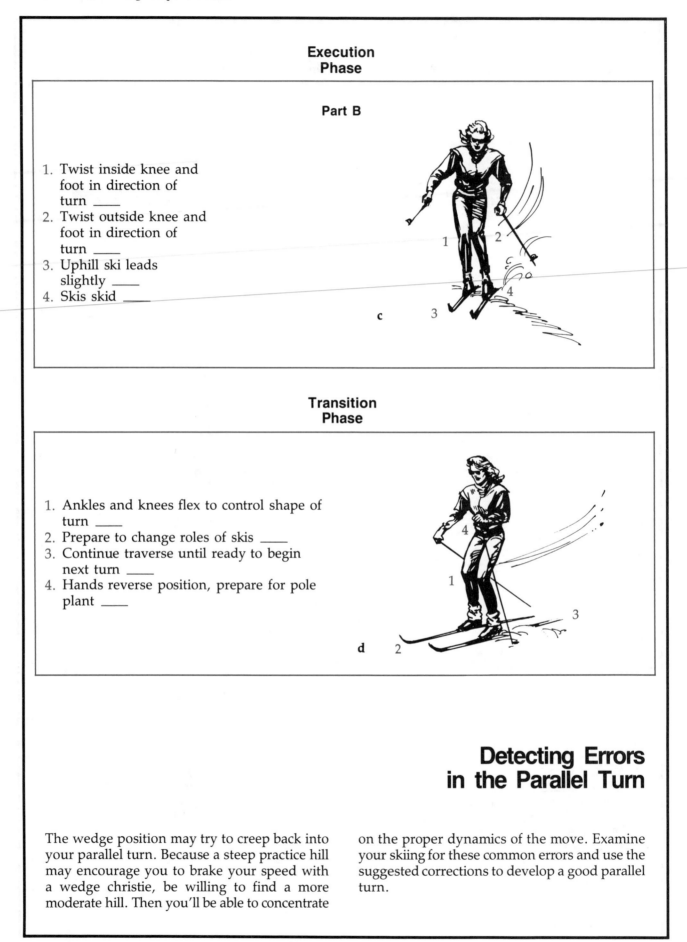

Transition
Phase

1. Ankles and knees flex to control shape of turn ____
2. Prepare to change roles of skis ____
3. Continue traverse until ready to begin next turn ____
4. Hands reverse position, prepare for pole plant ____

Detecting Errors
in the Parallel Turn

The wedge position may try to creep back into your parallel turn. Because a steep practice hill may encourage you to brake your speed with a wedge christie, be willing to find a more moderate hill. Then you'll be able to concentrate on the proper dynamics of the move. Examine your skiing for these common errors and use the suggested corrections to develop a good parallel turn.

ERROR 🚫	CORRECTION
1. Your narrow stance interferes with good balance.	1. Keep the skis under your hips for good side-to-side stability.
2. A wedge creeps back into your parallel stance.	2. Choose a more moderate hill to increase your comfort with the speed of the descent. Steer the inside ski first, and let it lead the outside ski through the turn.
3. Stiff ankles and knees create a tense stance.	3. Relax your ankles and knees with an exaggerated flex and extension. Use up-and-down motion to help turn.
4. Your skis skid excessively and wash out at the end of the turn.	4. Keep your torso upright and faced toward the fall line on steeper hills. Tilt your torso and hips forward down the hill into the next turn.

Fine-Tuned Turning Drills

1. Mock Wedge-Christie Drill #1

Stand on flat terrain at the top of the hill with your skis in a wide parallel stance. Flex and extend at your ankles to loosen your legs. Begin the drill from a bent-ankle position. Stand tall, and slide one ski into wedge position. Lift the other ski, and let it skim across the snow. Place it parallel to the ski you're standing on. Flex at the ankles and knees again to lower your center of gravity. Exaggerate the up-and-down motion to keep your legs flexible.

Success Goal = 10 mock wedge christies with exaggerated vertical motion

Your Score = (#) _____ mock wedge christies

2. Wedge-Christie Garland Drill

Begin this drill from a traverse across a wide hill. Move into a gliding wedge turn. Stand tall, shift weight to the outside ski, and steer the inside ski into parallel alignment. Steer your skis into the hill and come to a complete stop.

Repeat the sequence, and create a garland of wedge christies in the same direction as you turn continuously into the hill.

In preparation for a turn in the other direction, return to Drill #1 to practice the mock christie. Then repeat Drill #2 to perform the garland in the new direction.

Success Goal = 10 linked wedge christies in a garland

  a. 5 christies to the right

  b. 5 christies to the left

Your Score =

    a. (#) ＿＿ wedge christies in garland to the right

    b. (#) ＿＿ wedge christies in garland to the left

3. Mock Wedge-Christie Drill #2

Repeat Drill #1, but extend the sequence by stepping into a wedge christie in the other direction. This sequence mimics the steps in linked wedge christies. Continue the transitions from "turn" to "turn" to develop rhythmic up-and-down action of the body.

Success Goal = 6 mock wedge christies with rhythmic vertical motion

Your Score = (#) ＿＿ mock wedge christies

4. Linked Wedge-Christie Drill

Precede this drill with a series of smoothly linked gliding wedges. In the second descent, use wedge christie turns to descend the hill.

    Stay in the wedge turn until you have traveled through the fall line. Then stand tall, lighten the inside ski, and steer your inside ski into parallel alignment with the outside ski. Reverse the roles of your skis in the next turn.

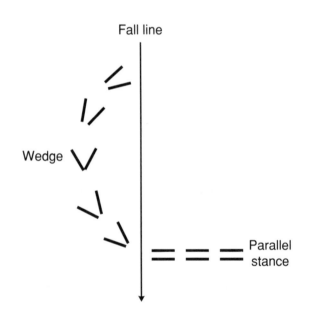

Success Goal = A series of linked wedge christies with a shallow arc

Your Score = (#) ＿＿ linked wedge christies with a shallow arc

5. Decreasing Wedge Drill

Practice a series of wedge turns, using a wedge shape narrower than the one used in the preceding drill. The transition to parallel turns is enhanced when you begin to decrease the size of the wedges.

    Descend the hill with linked wedge christies that flow from this new wedge shape. To be comfortable with the increased speed, steer your skis more strongly into the hill at the end of the turn. This stronger steering creates wider, rounder turns.

    Ask a friend to observe the wedge shapes to make sure the wedge remains narrower.

Success Goal = A series of linked wedge christies from a narrower wedge

Your Score = (#) ＿＿ linked wedge christies from a narrower wedge

6. Before-the-Fall-Line Drill

Use a series of linked wedge christies to descend the hill. Move more quickly from the wedge initiation to the parallel position by changing the location at which you begin to match your skis. As you steer around the arc of the turn, steer the inside ski into position before the fall line.

Your speed increases as both skis enter the fall line, but finish off the turn with an exaggerated bending of your ankles and knees to enhance balance. Roll your ankles and knees into the hill to control the skid at the completion of the turn.

Eventually you match your skis earlier and earlier in the turn until the wedge happens for a fleeting moment.

Success Goal = Parallel matching of your skis prior to the fall line

Your Score = (#) _____ wedge christies with earlier parallel matching

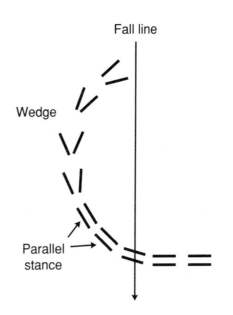

7. Pole-Plant Drill

Poling can help initiate the wedge christie turn. Lightly plant the downhill pole as you rise from the wedge, and steer around it. Think "touch-and-up." This leads the way for you to lighten your skis, and steer them around the corner.

Keep your hands in front of your body about waist high to ready them for poling. Don't let the poling hand fall behind your body, as this will cause your torso to rotate through the turn. If your hand remains in front of your body, you can slide the pole easily into position with a flick of your wrist

Holding the grip of longer poles can force you into a high-hands position, which can send your weight backward. You can hold the pole shaft at a point so that your arm forms a right angle during the pole plant. This light grip also encourages you to rely on the plant as a timing device more than as a balance mechanism.

Success Goal = Light pole touches with wedge christies

Your Score = (#) _____ light pole touches

8. Swivel Drill

Stand in place with your skis in a wide parallel stance under your hips. Smooth, well-groomed snow is helpful for this exercise. Plant your poles to the side of the skis for balance. Keep your legs flexed at the ankles and knees.

Think of your shinbones as central axes, and rotate your feet around them. Let your knees swing to enhance the foot rotation. The skis swivel simultaneously with this two-footed steering. Swivel the skis until you can rotate them 5 times in a parallel stance.

Success Goal = 5 swivels in a parallel stance

Your Score = (#) _____ swivels in a parallel stance

9. *Hockey Stop Drill*

Stand tall in a wide, parallel stance, and glide down the hill (see Figure a). Let your speed aid the turn. Drop your weight sharply with an exaggerated bend at your ankles and knees. Steer both skis simultaneously through the fall line. Keep your torso facing down the fall line as you skid to a stop (see Figure b). Practice this hockey stop in both directions. If you have difficulty turning to one side, focus on the inside foot and twist it first to steer the skis around.

a

b

Success Goal = 2 hockey stops in opposite
    directions

Your Score =

   a. (#) _____ 1 hockey stop to the right

   b. (#) _____ 1 hockey stop to the left

10. *Sideslipping Drill*

Prepare to sideslip downhill. Stand tall and move your knees away from the hill to release the edges and slide sideways. Keeping the skis parallel, sink lower and prepare to come to a stop. Your knees swing toward the hill to edge your skis and control the skid.

Continue to move down the hill. Stand tall again to release the edges, and repeat the process until you can feel strong two-legged steering.

Return to the top of the hill, and repeat the exercise by following a more diagonal line down the hill. Point your skis toward the fall line only as much as feels comfortable when sideslipping. You have to steer your skis more strongly by directing your toes and knees into the hill to stop the sideslip.

Descend the hill a third time by pointing your skis closer to the fall line. As you near the fall line in initiating these moves, your actions intensify. Speed increases as you point your skis downhill. Increase the bending at your ankles and knees, and move your toes and knees strongly into the hill to steer the skis.

Success Goal = 3 descents with turns progressively closer to the fall line

    a. 1 descent with sideslipping across the fall line

    b. 1 descent with sideslipping diagonally toward the fall line

    c. 1 descent with sideslipping close to the fall line

Your Score =

    a. (#) _____ descent across the fall line

    b. (#) _____ descent diagonal toward the fall line

    c. (#) _____ descent close to the fall line

11. Inside-Knee Parallel Drill

Point your skis down the fall line in a wide stance, and steer them through a turn by leading with your inside knee. This action directs your inside knee and inside big toe into the turn. Follow this steering with a corresponding action from your outside ski. This focus keeps your inside leg a very active part of the necessary two-footed steering and prevents it from falling behind.

    Complete the turn, stand tall, and let your flattened skis begin sliding downhill in the direction of the next turn. Initiate the steering by moving your inside knee into the turn again. Although the inside leg leads, the lag between it and the outside leg is almost imperceptible.

Success Goal = Linked wide-stance parallel turns

Your Score = (#) _____ wide-stance parallel turns

Fine-Tuned Turning Keys to Success Checklists

Mastering these advanced turns requires a more complex combination of skills. It's difficult to make improvements without assistance from an instructor, a coach, or a knowledgeable skier.

Ask your observer to use the checklists in Figures 12.1 and 12.2 to observe your performance and provide effective feedback.

Step 13 **Accelerated Skating**

Turning on steeper hills helps you become comfortable with using your legs independently, and your one-legged balance increases dramatically. You're now ready for more aggressive skating maneuvers where you glide longer on your skis.

V-skating on flat terrain can be an exhilarating proposition, because you ski powerfully and quickly across the snow. The sensation of flying lightly over bumps and dips in the terrain is a pleasurable one with these moves.

Two V-skating maneuvers are appropriate at this point in your development: V2 and V2 Alternate. They require some subtle modifications to the skating maneuvers that you have already learned.

In V2-skating, you double pole twice for every two skates. In other words, every time you skate onto a ski, you must also double pole over it. But the timing changes from the marathon skate and V1-skating, where the poling and skating were synchronized. Here the timing is staggered. You skate onto the ski, and then pole.

V2 Alternate requires only one double-poling motion for every two skates, as in V1. The timing of V2 Alternate differs from V1 and uses the staggered timing of V2. You skate onto one ski, double-pole over it, skate onto the other ski without poling, and skate back to your original ski (where you double-pole again to repeat the sequence). Confused? Just think of the move as V1-skating with delayed poling.

WHY IS THE V2 SKATE IMPORTANT?

The staggered timing of V2-skating lets you generate momentum more consistently over flat terrain. Because you skate and then pole, you propel yourself forward first with your leg and then with your poling. There is little lag in your forward momentum.

In contrast, the synchronized timing of V1-skating creates a burst of power on one side, effective for climbing hills, but less momentum when you skate onto the nonpoling side. V2-skating is most effective on flat terrain and transitions to downhills, but advanced skiers also use it to begin climbing hills. They carry their momentum through the transition at the bottom of the hill with V2-skating and then switch to V1 only when they need more power to climb uphill.

V2-skating is also relaxing, in that your tempo can slow. You glide longer on each ski, riding out the additional speed generated by the double poling, before you skate onto the other ski. Once your comfort with one-ski gliding has improved, you will find this longer skate to be very rewarding.

WHY IS V2 ALTERNATE IMPORTANT?

V2-skating can be so powerful, especially with fast snow conditions, that your poling may begin to interfere with your balance. Additional acceleration from poling is no longer required. V2 Alternate is an important option at this point. Simply omit one of the poling actions from the V2, and pole once for every two skates—that's V2 Alternate. You'll have better balance as you ride out the speed.

Your speed may continue to increase, especially as you descend a dip in the terrain. You can omit both poling actions to maintain your balance and comfortable momentum. Now you've changed into no-pole skating, introduced in Step 4. If your speed starts to subside, then reintroduce some poling for an extra burst of power.

The addition of V2 and V2 Alternate, with their alternate timing, provides you with a wide range of skating maneuvers from which to choose. Tailor your skating to the terrain, your strength, and the speed of your skiing. Let your maneuvers flow together, and be ready to change them to suit the situation. The virtue of this family of V-skating moves is their great versatility, which makes you a more versatile skier.

HOW TO EXECUTE THE V2 SKATE

Reinforcing the timing of the V2 skate is an important objective in your learning. Skate and pole more passively at the outset until you are comfortable with the timing; otherwise the power of this maneuver will upset your balance.

Skate forward onto one ski (see Figure 13.1, a and b). Ride this gliding ski with your hips high and forward in preparation for a crisp double-poling action. Swing your arms forward over this gliding ski (see Figure 13.1c). Just before your momentum subsides, double-pole over the skating ski with slight compression of the torso (see Figure 13.1, d and e). Glide speed at this point is often so fast that a deep compression for extra power is unnecessary.

Align the pendular swing of your arms with the ski. Your hands can actually follow the outside edges of the ski as they push down and backward. When your hands approach your thighs, skate onto the other ski. Let your poling follow through behind your body as you complete the torso compression accompanying the poling (see Figure 13.1e).

Then return the poles over this new skating ski, while raising your torso and bringing your hips high and forward again (see Figure 13.1f). Let your hands frame the ski as they move to approximately chin level. This position helps keep you centered over the gliding ski and ready for effective double poling. Double-pole again, and repeat the same sequence (see Figure 13.1g).

Remember the staggered timing with this cadence: skate-and-pole, skate-and-pole. Include the word ''and'' in the sequence to encourage you to ride the gliding ski longer before you pole. Initially, you might tend to rush the timing by poling too soon, if you are uncomfortable riding the gliding ski. It may be beneficial to repeat the one-ski gliding exercises in Step 1.

Figure 13.1 Keys to Success: V2 Skate

Preparation Phase

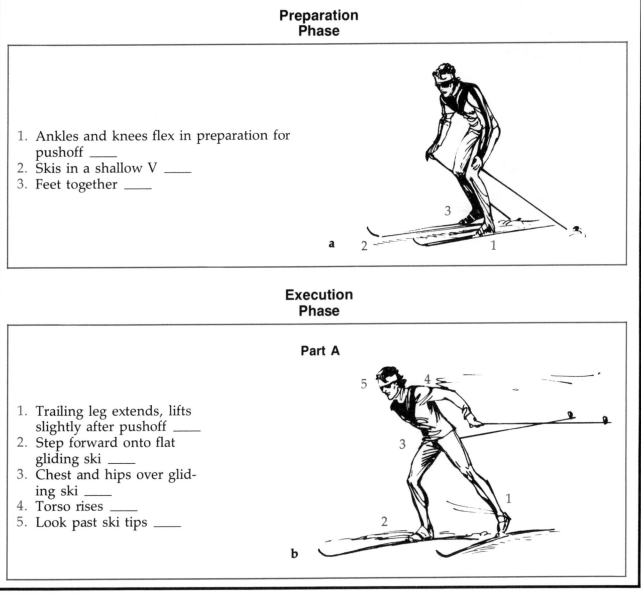

1. Ankles and knees flex in preparation for pushoff ____
2. Skis in a shallow V ____
3. Feet together ____

Execution Phase

Part A

1. Trailing leg extends, lifts slightly after pushoff ____
2. Step forward onto flat gliding ski ____
3. Chest and hips over gliding ski ____
4. Torso rises ____
5. Look past ski tips ____

Execution
Phase

Part B

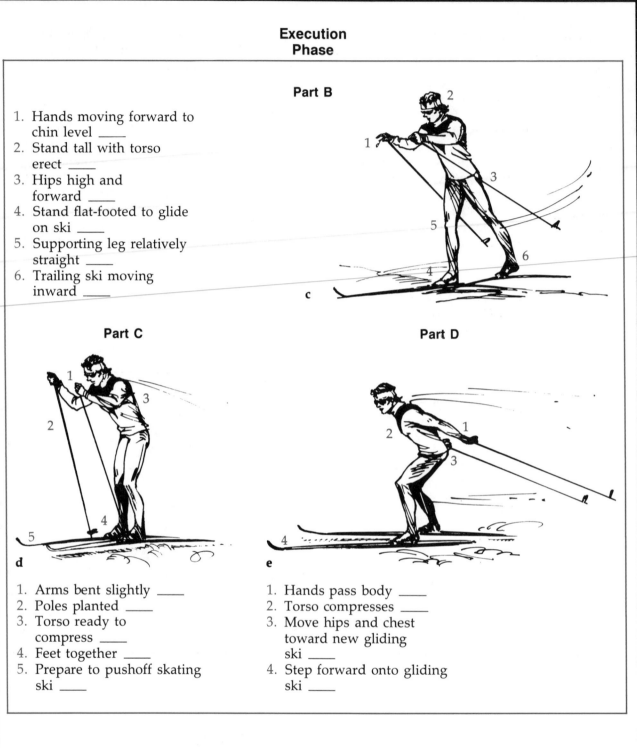

1. Hands moving forward to chin level ____
2. Stand tall with torso erect ____
3. Hips high and forward ____
4. Stand flat-footed to glide on ski ____
5. Supporting leg relatively straight ____
6. Trailing ski moving inward ____

c

Part C

d

1. Arms bent slightly ____
2. Poles planted ____
3. Torso ready to compress ____
4. Feet together ____
5. Prepare to pushoff skating ski ____

Part D

e

1. Hands pass body ____
2. Torso compresses ____
3. Move hips and chest toward new gliding ski ____
4. Step forward onto gliding ski ____

Execution Phase

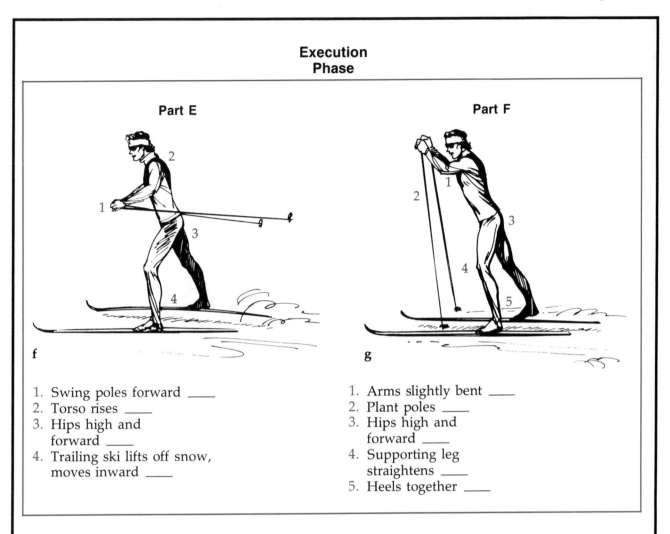

Part E

f

1. Swing poles forward ____
2. Torso rises ____
3. Hips high and forward ____
4. Trailing ski lifts off snow, moves inward ____

Part F

g

1. Arms slightly bent ____
2. Plant poles ____
3. Hips high and forward ____
4. Supporting leg straightens ____
5. Heels together ____

Detecting Errors in the V2 Skate

The timing of the skating and poling is important. It must be staggered so that you can generate more consistent momentum throughout the move. Your comfort in gliding on one ski is also a factor. You may benefit from a repeat of the one-ski glide exercises in Step 1 to improve your comfort. Common errors with suggested corrections are listed in this section.

ERROR

CORRECTION

1. Poor balance creates short, wobbly gliding.

2. Skating onto the ski is followed almost immediately by double poling. A fast tempo results.

1. Practice the one-ski gliding exercises in Step 1 so you can center your body comfortably over the ski.

2. Improve your balance so you aren't tempted to use your poling immediately to aid balance. Take time to ride your gliding ski.

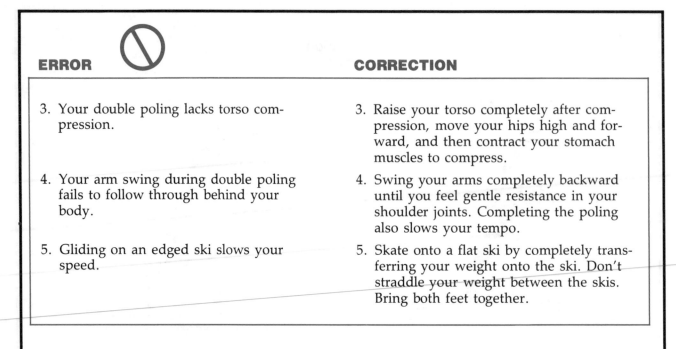

ERROR	CORRECTION
3. Your double poling lacks torso compression.	3. Raise your torso completely after compression, move your hips high and forward, and then contract your stomach muscles to compress.
4. Your arm swing during double poling fails to follow through behind your body.	4. Swing your arms completely backward until you feel gentle resistance in your shoulder joints. Completing the poling also slows your tempo.
5. Gliding on an edged ski slows your speed.	5. Skate onto a flat ski by completely transferring your weight onto the ski. Don't straddle your weight between the skis. Bring both feet together.

HOW TO EXECUTE V2 ALTERNATE

V2 Alternate is an easy extension of the V2 skate. You can ski across flat terrain with V2 and simply eliminate one of the poling motions from the sequence to initially learn the rhythm. Slow down the return swing of your poles, because you don't need to bring them over the new skating ski to pole. Skate out and leave your arms behind your body. Recover your poles when you skate onto the poling ski.

If this approach is confusing, then begin slowly from a standing position. Step diagonally forward onto one ski, and swing your arms forward over this poling side (see Figure 13.2, a and b). Stand tall on the gliding ski, bringing your trailing foot inward for a tight stance, and raise your poles to chin level (see Figure 13.2c). Push down on the poles, and compress your torso slightly to continue momentum (see Figure 13.2d). As your hands approach your body, skate onto the nonpoling ski. Let your arms swing behind your body as you ride the flat ski (see Figure 13.2e).

Continue to ride this nonpoling ski as you begin to recover your poles and prepare to repeat the sequence (see Figure 13.2f). Use this pole recovery to raise your torso and move your hips high and forward over the poling-side ski. This action centers your body over the gliding ski, enhances momentum, and puts you in an aggressive posture to begin double poling again.

You can use this cadence to reinforce proper timing of the poling and skating: skate-pole-skate-skate-pole. Saying this phrase will help you eliminate one of the poling actions.

Figure 13.2 Keys to Success:
V2 Alternate

**Preparation
Phase**

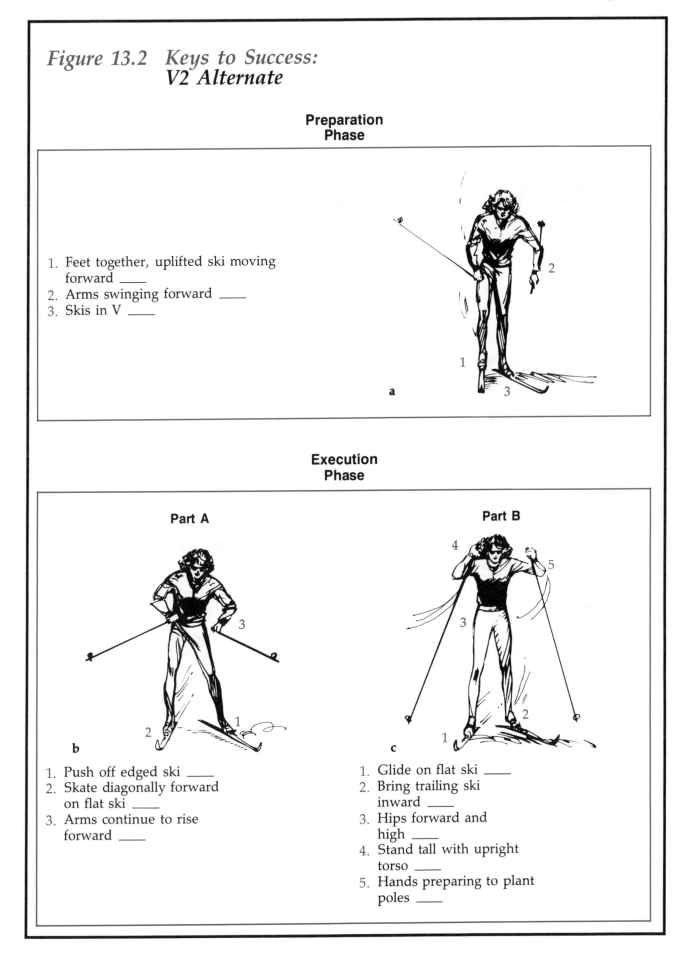

1. Feet together, uplifted ski moving
   forward ____
2. Arms swinging forward ____
3. Skis in V ____

**Execution
Phase**

Part A

b

1. Push off edged ski ____
2. Skate diagonally forward
   on flat ski ____
3. Arms continue to rise
   forward ____

Part B

c

1. Glide on flat ski ____
2. Bring trailing ski
   inward ____
3. Hips forward and
   high ____
4. Stand tall with upright
   torso ____
5. Hands preparing to plant
   poles ____

Execution Phase

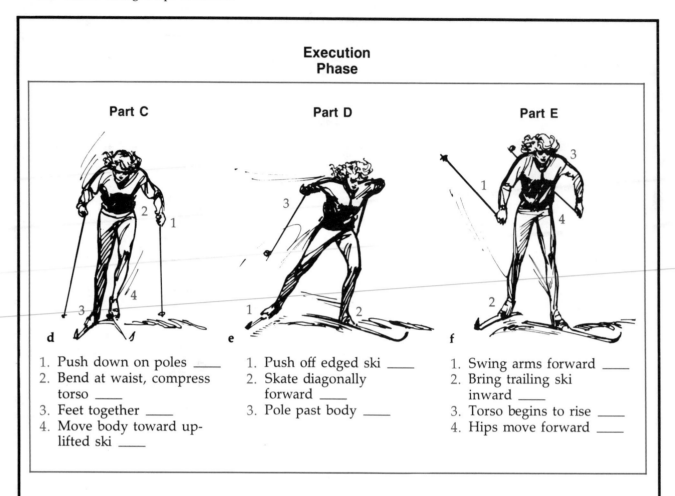

Part C

d

1. Push down on poles ____
2. Bend at waist, compress torso ____
3. Feet together ____
4. Move body toward uplifted ski ____

Part D

e

1. Push off edged ski ____
2. Skate diagonally forward ____
3. Pole past body ____

Part E

f

1. Swing arms forward ____
2. Bring trailing ski inward ____
3. Torso begins to rise ____
4. Hips move forward ____

Detecting Errors in V2 Alternate

Timing can also be a problem with V2 Alternate, because you may want to rush to get the poling back into the sequence. Starting from a stationary position and walking through the sequence of moves can be very helpful to reestablish the proper rhythm. Examine your skiing for these common errors, and use the recommended corrections to improve your performance.

ERROR

CORRECTION

1. Your poling and skating are more synchronized than staggered.

1. Improve your comfort with gliding on one ski to avoid early poling to enhance balance.

2. Your poles rush forward over the non-poling side and lag in the air.

2. Slow down your poling, and let your arms extend fully behind your body. Exaggerate the full extension. Return the poles over the power side.

ERROR ⃠	CORRECTION
3. Your arms extend away from your body during double poling, creating a wider and less powerful pendular swing.	3. Brush your arms down and close to the body during their pendular swing.

V2 and V2 Alternate Drills

1. Stationary V2 Drill

Stand in place with your poles held at midshaft. Angle one ski to make a V shape, and step on it. Completely transfer your weight to the ski, and raise your arms chest-high. Frame the length of the ski with the poles to center your body. Your hips should be high and forward. Bring the unweighted ski near the other ski with your feet close together.

Swing your arms down and back to mimic the poling. As your hands approach your body, step onto the other ski. Compress your torso, and let the poling continue behind your body. Recover your poles along the new skating ski, aligning the poles with the ski.

As the poles raise your torso also rises. Now mimic the double-poling motion again. As your hands approach your body, step back onto the other ski, and continue the sequence.

Develop a good rhythm as you step from ski to ski. Use this landmark to reinforce the timing: Step onto the new ski every time your hands brush past your body while poling. Continue your practice until you perform six complete mock V2 sequences. (A complete sequence is two poles and two skates.)

Success Goal = 6 sequences of mock V2 with proper timing

Your Score = (#) _____ sequences of mock V2 with proper timing

2. Step-and-Pole Walk Drill

Continue to hold the poles at midshaft to mock the poling. Repeat the sequence in Drill 1, but begin to walk forward through the drill. Step diagonally forward, then pole; step diagonally forward onto the other leg, then pole. This exercise also reinforces good staggered timing between poling and skating.

Continue to walk forward until you develop a consistent rhythm through 10 sequences of mock V2.

Success Goal = 10 consecutive forward steps of mock V2

Your Score = (#) _____ consecutive forward steps of mock V2

3. Two-Ski Glide Drill

This exercise uses double poling to reinforce V2 timing. It also simulates the path of V2, but lets you glide securely on two skis.

From a standing position, step both skis to one side and double-pole. Push down strongly on the poles, and compress your torso for good power. As your hands approach your body, step both skis in the opposite direction and continue to glide.

Continue the poling behind your body, and return the poles along the skis. Raise your arms and torso completely, and bring your hips high and forward. Begin to double-pole again, and step both skis in the other direction as your hands approach your body.

Continue double-poling in this V formation, and concentrate upon crisp double poling. Keep your hips forward at the beginning of the poling, because this practice will help to keep you balanced when you attempt the move on one ski.

Success Goal = 50 yards of crisp double poling in a V formation

Your Score = (#) _____ yards of crisp double poling in a V formation

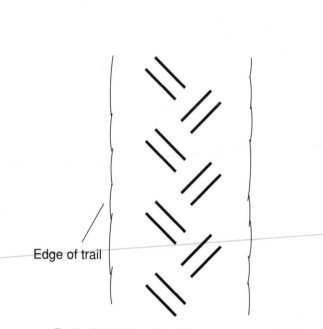

Edge of trail

Path of double poling down a groomed trail

4. Two-Ski-to-One-Ski Drill

Repeat the above exercise, and develop a consistent rhythm as you glide in the V formation. Whenever you feel comfortable with your rhythm, step onto only the outside ski as you move in a new direction. Then pole, and step onto only the outside ski in the other direction.

Whenever you become wobbly, place both skis on the snow to continue the sequence. Double-pole over both skis several times to recapture your rhythm, and step onto one ski only when it feels comfortable. Ski along a 50-yard course, and estimate how often you need the other ski for balance.

Ski the course again, and try to use only one ski at a time. Dampen your speed with lighter poling to help improve balance. Bring both feet together while gliding to also improve balance.

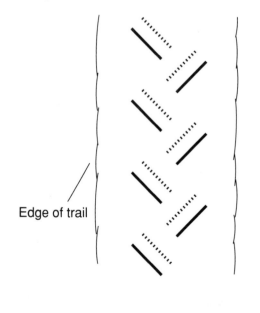

Edge of trail

Estimate how often you need to use two skis—
it should be much less!

Success Goal = A decreased number of
two-ski recoveries

Your Score =

a. (#) ____ two-ski recoveries during first run
b. (#) ____ two-ski recoveries during second
run

5. *Stand-Tall Drill*

Focus on your hips during this V2 practice. Each time you recover the poles prior to poling, stand tall on the ski with hips high and forward. A slight bend at the ankle lets you lean your entire body farther forward, like a figurehead on a ship. The unweighted foot hovers behind the front foot, acting as a counterbalance to your forward lean. This aggressive stance lets you snap your torso and arms downward for powerful double poling. A speedier V2 results.

Success Goal = 4 consecutive V2 sequences with powerful poling

Your Score = (#) ____ consecutive V2 sequences with powerful poling

6. *Toe-Off Drill*

Focus on your feet during this V2 practice. Slightly flex your ankle before pushing off the skating ski. The bend and extension provides extra power to help propel you onto the new skating ski. Your toe points if you have extended your ankle fully during pushoff. Immediately bring this foot inward to the skating foot to enhance balance over the skating ski. Think "toe-off" during the drill, and match it to the pushoff: toe (flex)–off (extend).

Experiment with varying degrees of pushoff, and watch their effects upon the extent of your glide. In soft snow, you can examine your tracks and witness how stronger pushoff gives you longer glide.

Success Goal = A comparison of weak and strong pushoff

Your Score = ____ Your judgment: Do you notice the variation in pushoff?

7. *Stationary V2 Alternate Drill*

Practice the timing of V2 Alternate in this stationary exercise. Hold the poles at midshaft to mimic the poling. Step onto an angled ski, and raise your arms chest-high. Swing your arms downward, keeping the poles parallel to the skis, and bend at the waist to compress your torso. As your arms approach your body, step onto the other ski, which is also angled. Continue poling past your body.

Prepare to step back in the other direction by returning your poling in that direction. Once your arms pass your body, raise your torso and step onto the ski. Stand tall to begin double poling again.

Use this cadence to reinforce the timing: skate-pole-skate-skate-pole.

Success Goal = 6 sequences of mock V2 Alternate with proper timing

Your Score = (#) _____ sequences of mock V2 Alternate with proper timing

8. V2 Alternate Walk Drill

Walk through the V2 Alternate sequences to further reinforce the timing. Continue to hold the poles midshaft to mimic the double poling. Step diagonally forward, pole, step diagonally forward in the other direction, continue to pole behind your body, step onto the other ski (bringing the poles forward), and pole again.

Walk through this sequence until you develop a smooth rhythm. It's especially important to slow down the tempo of the double poling and extend the poles completely behind your body while you're stepping onto the second ski.

Success Goal = 10 consecutive forward steps of mock V2 Alternate

Your Score = (#) _____ consecutive forward steps of mock V2 Alternate

9. Glide-Pole Drill

Grip the poles for normal poling during this drill, and prepare to glide on your skis. Pole lightly at the outset to limit forward momentum and enhance balance. Use this cadence as you move: skate-pole-skate-skate-pole. Say the words out loud to reinforce the timing.

Success Goal = 50 yards of V2 Alternate with proper timing

Your Score = (#) _____ yards of V2 Alternate with proper timing

10. Hand-Touch Drill

This exercise focuses on the poling follow-through to enhance your timing. As you pole past your body, extend your arms fully rearward until you feel resistance in your shoulder joints. Let your hands touch together at the point of farthest extension. This touching is an exaggeration for the purpose of lengthening your poling phase.

Touch your hands together for five sequences of V2 Alternate. Then complete the practice with five regular double poles, maintaining full rearward extension.

Success Goal = 5 hand-touches followed by 5 regular double poles during V2 Alternate

Your Score =

a. (#) ___ hand touches

b. (#) ___ regular double poles

Accelerated Skating
Keys to Success Checklists

Ask an instructor, a coach, or a knowledgeable skier to observe your V2- and V2 Alternate skating. Have your observer check the timing first to make sure the poling and skating are staggered rather than synchronized, then analyze whether your stance is affecting your ability to glide on each skating ski. Have your observer use the checklists in Figures 13.1 and 13.2 to evaluate your performance and provide corrective feedback.

Rating Your Total Progress

You have now practiced every major maneuver in classical, freestyle cross-country skiing, and Nordic downhill skiing. These moves enable you to handle flat terrain as well as hills of varying pitches. You now have the knowledge and skills to explore many cross-country trails safely and enjoyably.

The joy in cross-country skiing is exploring the outdoors in the winter season through an aerobic sport that keeps you physically fit. You have the ability to participate at whatever level interests you—from recreational touring to amateur racing. As you mature as a skier, I hope you continue to seek assistance and feedback to refine and perfect your technique.

The following self-rating inventory allows you to judge your overall progress with each cross-country maneuver. Use it as a basis for continued improvement.

	Very good	Good	Okay	Poor
Warming Up				
How to fall safely	_____	_____	_____	_____
How to get up unassisted	_____	_____	_____	_____
Balance, stationary	_____	_____	_____	_____
Balance, moving slowly	_____	_____	_____	_____
Forward Momentum on Flat Terrain				
Diagonal stride, good timing with arms and legs	_____	_____	_____	_____
Double poling, compression of upper body	_____	_____	_____	_____
No-pole skating, balanced gliding on each ski	_____	_____	_____	_____
Moving Uphill Efficiently				
Sidestepping with secure edging	_____	_____	_____	_____
Herringbone with secure edging, upright stance	_____	_____	_____	_____
Traverse to herringbone, steep hill	_____	_____	_____	_____
Descending Gentle Hills Comfortably				
Sidestepping downhill	_____	_____	_____	_____
Straight run, sliding on parallel skis	_____	_____	_____	_____
Wedge, gliding to a stop	_____	_____	_____	_____
Wedge, braking to a stop	_____	_____	_____	_____
Wedge, stopping on demand	_____	_____	_____	_____
Changing Directions				
Wedge turn, to the left	_____	_____	_____	_____
Wedge turn, to the right	_____	_____	_____	_____
Linked wedge turns	_____	_____	_____	_____
Linked wedge turns, around obstacles	_____	_____	_____	_____
Step turn, to the left	_____	_____	_____	_____

	Very good	Good	Okay	Poor
Step turn, to the right	————	————	————	————
Skate turn, to the left	————	————	————	————
Skate turn, to the right	————	————	————	————

Improved Power on Flat Terrain

Kick double pole, pushing off with left leg	————	————	————	————
Kick double pole, pushing off with right leg	————	————	————	————
Marathon skate, pushing off with left leg	————	————	————	————
Marathon skate, pushing off with right leg	————	————	————	————
V2	————	————	————	————
V2 Alternate, poling on the left	————	————	————	————
V2 Alternate, poling on the right	————	————	————	————

Climbing Hills Quickly and Efficiently

Uphill diagonal stride, dynamic weight transfer	————	————	————	————
Diagonal V	————	————	————	————
V1, poling on the left	————	————	————	————
V1, poling on the right	————	————	————	————
V1, changing poling sides regularly	————	————	————	————

Descending Steeper Hills

Telemark turn, to the left	————	————	————	————
Telemark turn, to the right	————	————	————	————
Linked telemark turns	————	————	————	————
Wedge christie, to the left	————	————	————	————
Wedge christie, to the right	————	————	————	————
Wedge christie with pole plant	————	————	————	————
Linked wedge christies	————	————	————	————
Traverses with kick turns	————	————	————	————
Parallel turn, to the left	————	————	————	————
Parallel turn, to the right	————	————	————	————

Skier Safety Skills

Knowledge of trail etiquette	————	————	————	————
Matching skiing skills to terrain difficulty	————	————	————	————

Your Range of Skiable Terrain

Beginner trails	————	————	————	————
Intermediate trails	————	————	————	————
Advanced trails	————	————	————	————
Groomed snow	————	————	————	————
Ungroomed snow	————	————	————	————

Glossary

angulation—The bending of the body along its central axis that allows the legs and torso to lean in different directions.

Alpine skiing—A discipline that involves primarily downhill skiing techniques; the equipment affixes the entire foot to the ski.

balancing on one ski—One of the most essential skiing skills; the skier is centered over one ski.

christie—A skidded turn in which both skis skid on the same edges at some point in the turn.

counterrotation—A difference in pivoting actions between the torso and the legs. The torso turns one way, while the legs turn the opposite way.

cross-country downhill skiing—A blend of Alpine and Nordic skiing moves also known as ''telemarking.'' The equipment blends metal-edged skis with a three-pin binding.

diagonal V—A skating maneuver to glide aggressively uphill with the skis in a V-shaped position.

diagonal stride—The most common cross-country maneuver for gliding across flat terrain and up hills. The term refers to the alternate arm and leg actions similar to walking.

double poling—A maneuver in which both arms push on the poles simultaneously to provide forward momentum. The upper body follows the arms to provide extra energy.

edging—A skill in which the skier tips the ski onto its edge causing it to dig into the snow. The greater the tilt of the ski, the greater the edging.

fall line—The imaginary line that follows the greatest angle of the slope.

garland—A pattern of turns across a hill that resembles a garland on a Christmas tree. The turns are consecutive and in the same direction.

gliding herringbone—A maneuver to slide uphill with skis in a V-shaped position.

herringbone—A maneuver to step uphill with the skis in a V-shaped position. A half herringbone uses a modified or half-V position.

kick double pole—Double poling combined with an extra push from the leg; also known as a single-step double pole. The swing of the leg provides more power than double poling alone.

maneuver—A combination of skills that create a more complex movement on snow.

marathon skate—Double poling combined with an extra push from an angled or skating ski. The technique is used in ski tracks to gain extra power.

moving from ski to ski—A skill that involves the transfer of weight from one ski to the other. Complete weight transfer occurs when the skier is centered over one ski at a time.

Nordic skiing—A discipline that involves cross-country and downhill maneuvers. The equipment affixes the toe to the ski and leaves the heel free.

parallel turn—A turning technique where the skis remain in a parallel or side-by-side stance from beginning to end.

poling—A skill where a planting of the poles increases a skier's momentum or guides a skier through a turn; a timing device that aids rhythmic skiing.

power side—The ski over which the poling occurs in skating moves.

pushing off—A skill that creates good traction and propels a skier forward; also known as gripping, because the ski's wax pocket grips the snow to create traction; also known as the kick in skiing.

sideslipping—A skidding of the skis to the side and forward down the hill.

sidestepping—Moving sideways by lifting one ski at a time across the snow.

single-step double pole—A technique that combines double poling with an extra push from the leg; also known as a kick double pole. The swing of the leg provides more power than double poling alone.

skate turn—A turning technique where a skier can accelerate around corners using a V-shaped position with the skis. The skier steps off one ski, steps onto the diverging ski, and brings the other ski parallel.

skating (no poles)—A maneuver to provide forward momentum where the skis form a V or angled shape. The skier steps off one ski, glides onto the diverging ski, and then glides back to the original ski.

skidding—A skill in which the skis slip sideways or around the snow.

skill—A simple action or task that is part of a more complex move; proficiency in performing a task.

steering—A skill where the rotary force of the leg and foot turns the ski.

straight run—A maneuver where the skier slides downhill in a relaxed, centered stance. The skis are parallel.

telemark turn—The oldest turning maneuver; the skier sinks into a curtsy, and the skis form one long curve to carve a stable turn.

V1—A skating maneuver that combines double poling with skating. The skier poles only once for every two skating steps. The move is used on groomed snow with no tracks.

V2—A fast skating technique that combines double poling with skating. The skier poles twice for every two skating steps. The move is used on groomed snow with no tracks.

V2 Alternate—A skating technique similar to V2, except poling occurs once for every two skating steps. Skating and poling are not synchronized as in V1.

wedge—A fundamental downhill maneuver to control speed. The skier angles the skis inward in an A shape and presses them against the snow; also known as the snowplow. A braking wedge is wider, with the skis edged more aggressively against the snow. A gliding wedge is narrower, with the skis flatter to the snow.

wedge turn—A turning maneuver with the skis in an A-shaped position. Linked wedge turns are usually gliding wedges, where the narrower width makes it easier to begin and end the turn.

About the Author

Laurie Gullion, one of America's top ski instructors, is an examiner for the Eastern Professional Ski Instructors of America (PSIA–E). She is responsible for leading instructor training clinics and certification exams in Nordic skiing. She has also worked as the PSIA–East Nordic Coordinator. When she's not busy with PSIA, Laurie works as an outdoor education specialist at Greenfield Community College in Massachusetts. This one-year certification training qualifies adults to conduct outdoor programs.

Laurie has written many books, including *Ski Games* from Leisure Press, and has published numerous magazine articles for *Canoe*, *Cross-Country Skier*, and *The American Canoeist*. Laurie holds a master's degree in sports management from the University of Massachusetts at Amherst. She also is a part-time lecturer in the sport studies program and teaches writing to sport management majors at the University of Massachusetts.

In her leisure time, Laurie enjoys wildflower photography, wilderness whitewater canoeing, travel, and training for physical fitness.